NORTH TO THE CAPE

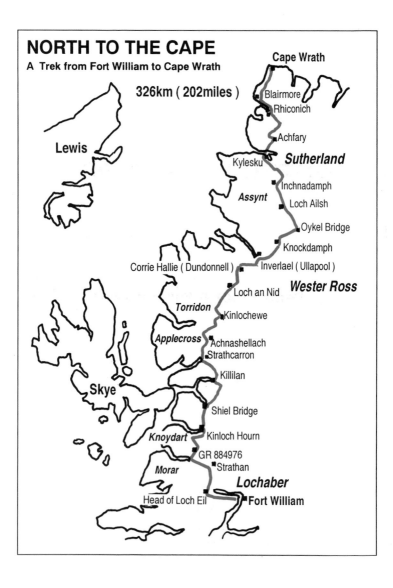

NORTH TO THE CAPE
A Trek from Fort William to Cape Wrath

326km (202miles)

Cape Wrath

Blairmore
Rhiconich

Achfary

Sutherland

Lewis

Kylesku

Inchnadamph
Loch Ailsh

Assynt

Oykel Bridge

Knockdamph

Corrie Hallie (Dundonnell)   Inverlael (Ullapool)

Wester Ross

Loch an Nid

Torridon

Kinlochewe

Applecross

Achnashellach
Strathcarron

Killilan

Skye

Shiel Bridge

Knoydart   Kinloch Hourn

GR 884976
Strathan

Morar

Lochaber

Head of Loch Eil   Fort William

NORTH TO THE CAPE

A Trek from
Fort William to Cape Wrath

by
Denis Brook & Phil Hinchliffe

CICERONE PRESS LTD
MILNTHORPE, CUMBRIA, U.K

ISBN 1 85284 285 7
A catalogue record for this book is available from the British Library.

ACKNOWLEDGEMENTS

Grateful thanks are offered to all those who, in one way or another, have contributed to the compilation of this book.

Very special appreciation goes to Sheila Banks, a close friend of both the authors, who became our 'grammar technician', 'road manager' and, as if that were not enough, wrote several poems to celebrate our travels; her counsel and encouragement were invaluable. We are indebted to our publishers, for their advice on many aspects of our work, and to Brian Evans, our printer, for his guidance on legibility and layout.

Our gratitude goes to Lynda Woods, General Secretary, and other members of the Mountain Bothies Association for their information and guidance on bothies. Assistant Secretary, Janet Clark, and members of the Scottish Rights of Way Society were kind enough to offer help and advice on Public Rights of Way. We thank Anne Mc Cranor, daughter of Denis Brook, for her dedicated research into the Scottish Monarchy, and Christine Dodds, a Highland landlady, for information on midges, clegs, ticks and flies.

Tourist Information Offices provided help with reference sources and the Scottish Youth Hostels Association kindly assisted with information on locations of hostels. Caledonian MacBrayne let us have details of their activities, as did Highlands and Islands Enterprise.

Finally, our grateful thanks go to the innumerable hoteliers, shop keepers, restaurateurs and members of the public who assisted us with advice, directions and encouragement.

Advice to Readers

Readers are advised that whilst every effort is taken by the authors to ensure the accuracy of this guidebook, changes can occur which may affect the contents. A book of this nature with specific descriptions is more prone to change than others. Waymarking alters, there may be new buildings or eradication of old buildings. It is advisable to check locally on transport, accommodation, shops etc but even rights-of-way can be altered, paths can be eradicated by landslip, forest fires or changes of ownership. The publisher would welcome notes of any such changes for future editions.

Other Cicerone books by the same authors:
> Alternative Pennine Way
> Alternative Coast-to-Coast

Front cover: The Cape. Image produced on an Apple Macintosh PowerBook G3 using Bryce 3D and Corel Draw 8

CONTENTS

PREFACE

In 1983, we walked from Cape Wrath to Fort William, with no navigational preparation other than a pencil line drawn over the relevant OS maps. We had a wonderful seventeen days with some sun and very little rain, staying at hotels, B & Bs or in a tent. We had dreams of writing up the adventure as a travelogue or as a guide, but the exigencies of careers and families took precedence.

Now, fifteen years later, having written *The Alternative Pennine Way* (APW), *The Alternative Coast to Coast* (ACC) and achieved retirement, we dusted off our dreams and returned to the route. This time we walked in the opposite direction - south to north; researched it in detail and made improvements. This guide is the result. We offer it to you, and hope that you get as much enjoyment, doing it your own way, as we did in walking and researching it.

INTRODUCTION

We make no apologies for the fact that this is a very tough walk, NOT to be attempted by inexperienced walkers. It might be the toughest long distance walk in the British Isles. This is NOT a walk where you learn walking skills; you've got to have all those before you start.

We will never please every walker's taste so we made the route to please ourselves. It proved impossible always to pass through places for accommodation etc. However, we did our best to satisfy the following criteria:

1. The route must pass through a variety of scenery.
2. It must avoid long hauls over featureless moors or along uninteresting straths.
3. It must use, as far as possible, designated paths whether or not they are defined on the ground.
4. It must pass, if possible, interesting geographical places.
5. It will be divided into stages, each one a good day's walk in length. If not ending at a place with accommodation, then it should end at a place where walkers can camp.
6. It must not pass, by design, over high peaks.

The consequences of 1 and 2 are that we chose to take the route through Knoydart, reputed to be the remotest part of Britain, and this meant going west from Fort William at the outset.

The journey starts at Fort William, crosses Loch Linnhe by ferry and meanders westerly beside Loch Eil. It then turns north through South Morar, North Morar and Knoydart, progressing over remote but beautiful countryside, visiting tiny hamlets on the way. Shiel Bridge, at the head of Loch Duich, provides a welcome break to replenish supplies. The Falls of Glomach, a breathtaking sight, precurses one's arrival at Strathcarron, the head of Loch Carron. The railway from Inverness to the Kyle of Lochalsh passes through here, affording an opportunity of breaking the journey. Through the Coulin Forest, a deer forest, and over the bealach (pass), the route reaches Kinlochewe, where the Beinne Eighe National Nature Reserve is situated. Liatach, Beinne Eighe, and Slioch dominate the area, a mecca for Munro baggers. Northwards, after passing An

Teallach, the route arrives within a few kilometres of Ullapool which, being the only large village north of Fort William, is well worth a visit. Over more bealachs and on to Oykel Bridge, beloved of anglers with the rivers flowing wide and deep, the countryside here is almost pastoral. Further north, the last of the Munros on this walk, Ben More Assynt, is skirted and the highest waterfall in Great Britain, Eas a Chùal Aluinn, is visited before reaching Reay (deer) Forest, the landscape being dotted with literally hundreds of lochans (small lochs). Then we go back to the west coast before negotiating the final stretch and arriving at the (usually) windswept headland of Cape Wrath.

The walk is split up into 21 Stages, each Stage being, as far as is possible, a good day's walk finishing where camping and perhaps accommodation is possible. Within the text, we have shown all the places known to us where provisions can be purchased. In several cases, we have provided details of alternative (Variant) routes — see General Notes. These are easier routes than the definitive ones and should prove helpful in bad weather conditions or if you wish to progress faster.

We would be disappointed if you followed our route slavishly, step by step. The route shown is the one we used. We hope that you will adapt this to suit your own circumstances.

In our previous books, the routes were designed to pass through hamlets and villages or towns, so that walkers could seek accommodation and provisions at will. THIS WALK DOES NOT FOLLOW THE SAME PATTERN! The reason for this is that the Western Highlands of Scotland are very sparsely populated. To include as many as possible of the inhabited areas would have made the route unnecessarily convoluted, and have included a lot of road walking. In consequence, this really is a quintessential backpacking walk. For those who prefer to minimise the backpacking element, we have indicated places where accommodation is possible. If you prefer an absolute minimum of backpacking, then persuade someone with a vehicle to support you. This has the double advantage that you carry fewer provisions and you sleep in a real bed most of the time. But NOT all of the time. Your driver(s) will enjoy the experience, perhaps as much as you, and we have shown relevant road heads in the text. It does not matter how you do this walk. The important thing is to do it and enjoy some of the world's most magnificent scenery.

We have visited many rare and beautiful places. We have marvelled at the magnificence of the Himalaya. We have been impressed by the Peruvian Andes and we have been moved by the sights of Mounts Kenya and Kilimanjaro. But, each time we visit the West Highlands, we conclude that this area cannot be surpassed for its mountains and valleys, its lakes and rivers, its remoteness and wild beauty. For us it is the best.

We offer no prizes to those who are the quickest to do this walk. Indeed, we would be more likely to commend those who are the slowest. It is an experience to be savoured and enjoyed to the utmost.

GENERAL NOTES

Preamble
If you have read thus far into this book, you will probably have done some walking in the Lake District, the Pennines and maybe Wales. Forget all that! The West Highlands of Scotland pose problems for walkers not encountered elsewhere. The vastness, the remoteness, the sparsity of its population, and thus accommodation and facilities, both add to its charm and will test the determination and skill even of the most experienced long distance walker. We offer, below, a few comments designed to set the scene, and some advice which may be helpful. We urge you to read and understand these Notes, the List of Symbols, the Definitions of Terms, all the Stage Maps and Notes, all the Navigation Maps and Notes, the Variants for the whole route and the Appendix "Leaving the Cape", before setting out on your great adventure.

Equipment
Far be it for us to describe to seasoned walkers what to wear and what to carry in your rucksack. This will depend to a great extent on how you propose to tackle the route. However, we emphasize that it is essential to wear strong, but not heavy, correctly fitting waterproof boots. Unless the weather is exceptionally favourable, you are going to get them very wet. For many years, we have been of the opinion that boots are the most important part of any walker's kit; get them wrong and your walk will be in jeopardy. Even if you have vehicular support, bivouac gear, at the very least a 'bivibag', should be carried in case timing is miscalculated. You will have nights out on the mountains, so camping equipment will be

necessary although, if you are very experienced, you may CHOOSE to bivouac. Emergency rations are obligatory. Each member of your party should carry a compass and map (see below), and know how to use them. And, naturally, first aid kits should be carried at all times. Every one of these items is particularly important in the Highlands of Scotland.

Maps and Navigation

The maps in this book must be regarded as sketch maps, but they should be accurate enough for *estimating* topography, distances, heights and directions for the whole journey. However, for precise observations, the OS Maps, which all self-respecting walkers carry, must be used. The relevant ones are listed in Appendix D. The hierarchy of our maps is as follows:

1. Frontispiece	Shows the whole route. North is at the top of the page.
2. Stage Maps	Twenty-one in total, which show each of the Stages. North is indicated by an arrow.
3. Navigation Maps	These are reproduced to a scale of approximately 1:50,000, to match closely the OS Landranger series. The National Grid is shown to facilitate easy transfer to OS maps. Also the one-kilometre squares will help in estimating distances. North is at the top of the page.

Bearings quoted are referenced to GRID NORTH, so remember the magnetic variation when transferring bearings to and from maps. All information was correct to the best of our knowledge at the time of research, but changes on the ground can occur, calling upon your own judgement.

During the Stalking Season (usually September/October), some routes may be closed (see Appendix B Public Rights of Way). In this event, notices will be displayed giving advice on alternative routes or suggesting that you contact the Head Stalker or Estate Factor. It's worth remembering that stalking seldom takes place on Sundays.

The information supplied on our maps should be more than adequate to guide you along the Definitive Route. The emphasis of presentation is graphical, that is by maps, and the words serve to clarify ambiguous points. We believe that the representation of a route, wherever it is, should be more than a description of a narrow corridor, as inevitable errors of navigation can easily be corrected if off-route information is to hand. Furthermore, too much detail can clutter the mind. The prime consideration is to know where you are and where you are aiming for. Then maps can be used, together with ground information, to achieve the objective. We hope that the maps and words in this book allow this to happen.

During our research we occasionally used a GPS (Global Positioning System) navigator, mainly to evaluate its effectiveness. We found ours useful to confirm positions, especially in cloud conditions. It is, of course, NOT necessary to carry and use one of these instruments. But if you do, it is absolutely critical to review and thoroughly understand all aspects of the operating instructions. Your instinct, coupled with your map reading and compass work, should tell you roughly where you are at all times. If the navigator appears to tell you something vastly different, then it is probably due to an error in usage.

Although shown on the maps, the way is not always evident on the ground so we have noted most of these areas in the text. Your own initiative, coupled with the information given, should ensure progress without difficulty, even in stressful conditions such as when time is short, when the weather is foul or when you are tired. It is situations such as these which highlight the real value of maps. All the information can be assimilated simultaneously, as distinct from facts presented serially in words. We feel that information like "turn right at the third stile by the signpost" is of dubious value, as the stile might now be a gate and the signpost may have fallen down or been removed.

Do NOT underestimate the time required to walk the Stages. You will know your own walking speed, but in 'Naismaith and Trantor' we offer some advice on timings. It is better to arrive early than late or not at all.

We realise that some people cannot come to terms with maps. We would strongly recommend that such people should NOT attempt this walk, unless accompanied by someone totally at home with them. This book is, without doubt, for the 'map person'.

There are no rights of way shown on OS maps relating to Scotland. Contrary to popular supposition, however, rights of way DO exist and these are sometimes shown on signs erected by the Scottish Rights of

Way Society (see Appendix B). Tales about access problems in Scotland abound, but we have never encountered real problems on any of our numerous visits.

Variant Routes

In 1983, when we walked from Cape Wrath to Fort William, we used some routes which differ from the definitive Fort William to Cape Wrath walk described in this guide. We have not used some parts of our original route for a number of reasons; mainly:

    a. To reduce the amount of road walking where possible, and

    b. Our definitive route has more variety and interest.

Information gained later, influenced these changes.

To make them easily understandable, we have described the Variants in a south to north direction.

Do note that we have not researched these routes since our 1983 walk, and the descriptions given are from memory and reference to OS maps. If you use any of the routes, you may find that, in places, the descriptions are at variance with reality. However, we suspect that the differences will be small enough to enable you, as skilled navigators, to find your way with little trouble.

The Variants in the main text are numbered to coincide with the Stage to which they refer. For instance: there is no Variant 1 but Variant 2 refers to Stage 2, Head of Loch Eil to Strathan. They are to be found at the ends of the Stages to which they refer, and their presence is indicated in the Stage Note titles.

Walking Groups

At the risk of stating the obvious, it would be most unwise to do a walk like this alone. Generally speaking, we like to walk as individuals or just the two of us. Principally, we like the calm of the open air and freedom from incessant conversation. At most, we walk in a party of three or four. This way, we can move through the countryside with the minimum of disturbance to groundcover and wildlife. And, you can see so much more when you are with only one or two companions. Also it's worth remembering that in the Scottish Highlands a large party might have difficulty with accommodation.

Accommodation

By its very nature, this walk passes through areas where accommodation is sparse or non-existent. If you are interested in hotels (and Scottish hotels can be very good and reasonably priced), guest houses and B & Bs, we advise that you make maximum use of the available publications listing such facilities and also that you use the Tourist Information Centres (TIC). The one at Fort William is open all year round. The ones at Ullapool and Durness are open from May to September, and the one at Shiel Bridge is open during 'the season' only. Any TIC will supply a map and directory listing the TICs in Britain. You should remember that not all accommodation is shown in the publications or registered with the TICs. But, we have found that one can usually find details of available accommodation simply by asking!

There are several bothies on the Definitive Route which we have, with one exception, NOT noted for the reasons explained in the 'Bothies and the MBA'. If you do use bothies, we entreat you to respect the Bothy Code printed there.

Cellphones

Once away from Fort William, cellphones were of no use in the West Highlands at the time of research. So if you were thinking of packing one in your bag, you may as well save some weight and leave it behind. Unless, at the time of your walk, the Highlands are 'on-line'.

Catering and Provisions

We have indicated most places where shops are to be found, but it is worth backpackers remembering that some weight can be saved by taking (some) meals, of the 'bar' variety perhaps, at hotels. Scottish hotels and guest houses are very welcoming and prepared to be flexible in their arrangements, so do not be afraid to find out in advance what is on offer.

Payment

In urban areas, we take for granted the use of bankers' credit and debit cards and sometimes forget that these facilities may not be available in all parts of the British Isles. A lot of places you will visit in Scotland have no shop, let alone a bank or cash dispenser. Forward-planning is therefore required, although most places will accept cheques supported by a cheque guarantee card.

Weather

There's plenty of it in Scotland! Do NOT assume that it will be fine tomorrow, or the next day, or the next day. We have known fourteen consecutive days of sunshine in Scotland. On the other hand, we have known fourteen consecutive days of rain. Make no mistake, your chances of getting wet are pretty high. There is no point in waiting for that elusive fine day. It may never happen. However, in order to take advantage of periods which MAY be dry, we suggest that you do the walk in April or May. Avoid July or August because of possible accommodation problems and midges. September and October can be fine, but remember that some routes may be diverted because of stalking activities. We offer no guarantees of fine weather at any time. We always assume that it will rain: if it doesn't, that's a bonus! Just make your choice and go for it.

River Crossings

We have designed this walk to avoid wading through any major rivers. But, depending on the weather, some wading may be necessary. On our trip in 1983, we had no problems whatsoever with any river crossing and we even kept our boots dry most of the time. During our research trips in 1997 and 1998, we had mixed fortunes. If you do come to a river that cannot easily be crossed, assess the situation very carefully. Several books about the techniques of walking offer advice on crossing rivers and, as experienced walkers, you will be well versed in the principles. However, we offer three tips:

1. If you are going to wade, then remove your socks and, if necessary, your trousers and store them where they cannot get wet.
2. Keep your boots on your feet. Do NOT attempt to cross in bare feet; you may injure yourself seriously.
3. Use a walking pole (see below).

It is obviously impractical to use the ideal equipment, anglers' waders. However, we have experimented with, and found to be advantageous, the use of strong plastic bags to enclose one's feet and lower legs; up to and above the knees at least. We wore the bags like long wellington boots, covering walking boots, socks and breeches; the bags being tied securely with cord around the legs above the knees. The cord was threaded through holes around the tops of the bags.

Walking is not easy with this equipment, but the use of a pole helps (see below). Even if the bags are pierced by sharp rocks, the ingress of water will not matter as the amount will be small due to the short time that you will be in the water. We emphasise that the bags must be strong; suitable rubble sacks can be purchased in good supermarkets.

Walking Poles

In our early walking careers, the use of poles (or sticks) as walking aids was unknown in this country, except for the elderly. Now, we realise their value; this realisation being reinforced by their popular use, even within the young walking fraternity.

Currently, we each use a single, stout, alpenstock-type wooden pole. They are just less than 1.25 metres long and about 30 millimetres in diameter. They have a wrist loop at the top and a brass ferrule at the bottom. We find them indispensable for providing a third point of support to increase stability; for testing boggy or snow covered ground for softness/hardness and depth; for fending off uncooperative dogs and inquisitive cattle and horses; for taking the strain off one's knees, especially when descending; and for steadiness when wading across rivers, particularly those with rocky beds or fast flowing water — or both. If pushed off balance by water, one can rely on the pole to take a lot of one's own weight as well as that of the rucksack.

The costs of these advantages are the extra weight and the encumbrance factor. They are a particular nuisance when scrambling either up or down, when one needs both hands free. It is not unknown for a pole, hanging on its wrist cord, to get between one's legs and impair movement. They are also a nuisance when operating a camera, especially at speed, or when wanting to handle, for purposes of examination, some wayside object. Despite these problems, we both still use a pole for rough walking. We do not use them when on an outing involving considerable scrambling or when walking on very easy terrain.

We are aware that many of the walking and climbing magazines carry advertisements for 'adjustable, antishock, telescopic, lightweight, carbon tipped poles, with interchangeable baskets etc'. The advertisers claim that 'professionals' use them and advocate the use of two poles at all times. We have little experience of these devices, double or single. But, because of the disadvantages noted above, compounded if two poles are used, we remain to be convinced of the value of two poles.

Finally

Whilst every effort has been made to represent the route accurately on the maps and to give correct descriptions, neither the authors nor the publisher can accept any responsibility in connection with any trespass or accident arising from the use of the definitive or variant routes or any associated route.

DEFINITION OF TERMS

Road
A way which is metalled and intended for normal motor vehicles.

Lane
A way along which a motor vehicle could be driven with care, but certainly a way on which a tractor would have no difficulty.

Track
A way along which walking is easy, even if the surface is rough, but along which a tractor would have difficulty.

Path
A way along which only walkers could pass (could also be a bridleway).

Trod
A way made by sheep or other animals, useful for walking.

N, SE etc.
Approximate bearings.

LIST OF SYMBOLS

Definitive Route (DR) shown on Ordnance Survey (OS)

DR shown in Scottish Hill Tracks, but not on OS

DR in open country

DR on road or track (fenced/unfenced)

Variants (Part of)

Other paths (*)

Metalled roads (fenced/unfenced)

Tracks (fenced/unfenced)

Rivers, burns

Contours (normally at 50-metre intervals)

Bridge (*)

Rock outcrops

Buildings

A B C   References to Map Notes

(*) Only shown when useful for navigation

SCOTLAND
A Brief History

There is a legend about a Spaniard on a visit to the Western Highlands. Discussing his own country over the odd dram with a Scottish friend, he was trying to explain the idea of *mañana*. He wasn't having much success, as his friend seemed unable to grasp the concept. "Well" said the Spaniard, "it means tomorrow, or the day after, or sometime". Suddenly his friend's face was aglow with enlightenment. Taking a careful sip of his dram, he said: "Now I understand. But there is no Gaelic word to express such a degree of urgency".

Apocryphal though this tale may be, the Scotland of today with its mountains, lochs and glens surrounded by 610 islands to the north, east and west, presents a picture of peaceful countryside inhabited by easygoing people. But that was not always the case, for Scotland has a long and turbulent history.

The earliest species of 'Homo', ancestors of modern man, came to Britain more than 2,500,000 BC when it was still part of the continental landmass. They were hunter-gatherers, using crude stone tools and weapons. Their settlements advanced and retreated with the glaciers of the four main Ice Ages. From around 11,000 BC, following a rise in temperature, the tundra-like vegetation gave way to forests and grasslands. Because of the melting ice, the sea level gradually rose, finally resulting in the cutting of the land bridge to the continent. Britain had become an island by about 6,500 BC, making migration more difficult for small groups and impossible for large ones.

Around 3,000 BC, Mesolithic hunters and fishermen began to settle in Scotland and by 2,000 BC Neolithic man was cultivating cereals and keeping cattle and sheep there. Seven hundred BC brought an identifiably final period to British prehistory, with the change from a relatively warm and dry climate to one which was cooler and wetter. Late Bronze Age and Early Iron Age Man changed activities from mixed farming to stock raising and began to safeguard their possessions, building hill forts.

The Roman occupation of Britain started in 56 AD. Whilst the Romans had a profound effect on life in England and Wales, they had little effect upon Scotland and made no impact upon the Western Highlands. Parts of Hadrian's Wall still stand, serving as a reminder of the Roman Empire's northern frontier. Some say it was built to satisfy the egomania of the Romans, whilst others think it was a means of surveillance and control as opposed to a deterrent against invasion.

In 406, after nearly four centuries of occupation, the Romans departed. There followed a long period, the Dark Ages and Medieval Ages, about which written information is scanty. The Picts, a Roman term for the people of Northern Scotland and possibly meaning 'painted or tattooed', occupied Scotland north of the Forth. The Scots, a Celtic people from Northern Ireland, colonised Argyll. Other Celtic Britons came to Scotland from the south and, from Northern Europe, the Angles created the Kingdom of Northumbria.

In 843, Kenneth Macalpin, King of the Scots, defeated the Picts adding their kingdom to his own. The Scots and the English were frequently attacked by the Vikings, and often combined forces to repel them. Edmund of England leased Cumbria to Malcolm I of Scotland in 945 as a gesture of friendship, and the Scots steadily pushed their boundaries north and east during the following 200 years. The Scottish monarchy which emerged during the 11th and 12th centuries theoretically created a united kingdom of Scotland. However, whilst wielding authority over the east and central Lowlands and the east coast, south of the Moray Firth, the power of this monarchy was weak in the Eastern Highlands and practically nonexistent in the Western Highlands.

Alexander III of Scotland died in 1286 and was succeeded by his three-year-old granddaughter Margaret. Her father was Eric II of Norway and she became known as the 'Maid of Norway'. Little Margaret died on her way to Scotland and, following her death, 13 claimants to the throne emerged, most of them wealthy, influential businessmen. In desperation, the Scottish barons turned to Edward I of England for a solution to the perplexing problem of succession. His appointment in 1292 of John Balliol to the Scottish throne proved to be a turning point in Scottish history. Edward used Balliol as a puppet ruler, hoping to further England's ambitions to rule the whole of Scotland. Scotland in general and the Borders in particular were plunged into wars of succession and independence. These lasted three centuries, ending in 1603 with the union of the crowns of Scotland and England.

Many bitter battles were fought. Carlisle was repeatedly attacked. Berwick changed hands 13 times. Towns and villages on both sides of the

Border became scenes of bloody conflict. In 1314, one battle between the English and Scottish armies became what many Scots regard as 'the greatest day in Scottish history'. It has also been described as a decisive battle of the world. Ten thousand of Robert the Bruce's men defeated 20,000 men of the English army at Bannockburn. This ended Edward II of England's chance of creating a united kingdom. At the Battle of Haliden Hill, in 1333, Edward III defeated the Scots, took Berwick and reined in the Borders to English control. Ten thousand Scots died in this conflict. In 1388 the Scots carried out a celebrated raid on Northumberland, the battle of Otterburn. It was fought 'in moonlight by heroes', resulting in a resounding victory for the Scots. The Earl of Douglas was killed defeating Henry Percy (Earl of Northumberland and Shakespeare's Hotspur), who was himself captured. One hundred Scots were killed and over 1,000 Englishmen were captured or killed. The Battle of Nisbet in 1402 was overshadowed by the great Battle of Homilden Hill in the same year. It was then England's turn to win a raid, this time on Newcastle, cutting off the Scots' retreat and putting them to flight, with deadly archery, at Wooler. The battles at Piperden in 1435 and Hedgeley Moor in 1464 were minor skirmishes compared with Flodden.

The Battle of Northumberland's Flodden Field in 1513 is perhaps the most famous of the Border battles. Thomas Howard, Earl of Surrey, led the English to a clear-cut victory. The English faced a Scots army twice its own size, but the experienced Thomas trounced the less worldly King James IV of Scotland with overwhelming fire power from cannon and bow. James was killed: so were 13 earls and up to 10,000 men. Attempting to take revenge for Flodden, the Scots fought the Battle of Solway Moss, near Carlisle, in 1542. Again, they were thoroughly defeated by a much smaller English force.

The many battles fought between the fourteenth and sixteenth centuries were formal events between the kingdoms of England and Scotland. There were, in addition, other lesser known skirmishes. Some Border families became notorious for ferocious raids on each other's property. Eventually, the Kings of England and Scotland agreed to divide up the frontier into the East, Middle and West Marches. Each March had one English and one Scottish warden who were supposed to confer about once a year and try to alleviate the problems brought about by these conflicts. It was not unknown, however, for the wardens themselves to take part in the raids.

On top of the private family feuds, much cattle, sheep and horse stealing took place. The wardens were obliged to try to control the offenders, but such was the frequency of the attacks that they were impotent. Aggrieved parties reported attacks to 'the authorities', but to little or no avail. An alternative was to resort to the 'Hot Trod'; the legal right to pursue the assailant and recover property, by force if necessary. The 'Hot Trod' had to be carried out within six days of the initial attack. If the border was crossed in pursuance of one's rights, then the 'Hot Trod' had to be proclaimed at the first village across the border. 'Hot Trodders' were often ambushed and taken prisoner, resulting in counter-attacks and counter-counter-attacks.

Partly for the defence of the kingdoms and partly in an attempt to stem the raiders, whose antics were a persistent menace to peace, defensive positions were erected on both sides of the Border.

The Stewart family ruled Scotland for 232 troubled years before James VI of Scotland succeeded Elizabeth I of England in 1603, uniting the two countries. James had ruled Scotland as despot for 25 years, manipulating the Scottish Parliament to his liking. The English Parliament made it quite clear that it did not support the 'divine right of kings' and eventually the Stuarts, as they had become known, accepted that they ruled by Parliament's consent.

In an attempt to obliterate old memories, James reduced the frontier fortresses and garrisons to peacetime levels and banned the use of the word 'Borders', hoping to substitute the designation 'Middle Shires'. But the familiarity and geographical accuracy of 'Borders' prevailed over the somewhat meaningless alternative.

The Border Wars over, Scotland still had problems. Attempting to bring about an end to the activities of Jacobite sympathisers, William III ordered all Scottish clan chiefs to swear an oath of allegiance to him and forsake their arms by 1 January 1692. Alexander Maclan MacDonald of Glencoe accidentally failed to meet the deadline and a punitive expedition was mounted by an old enemy, Campbell of Glenlyon, supported by a company of Argyll's regiment. On 13 February 1692, thirty-eight members of the MacDonald clan, including Alexander Maclan himself, were massacred at Glencoe. The survivors fled to the surrounding hills to suffer the rigours of a Highland winter.

The union of the crowns came about by inheritance, but the union of the two Parliaments was less easy. For many years the Scottish Parliament was of a mind to disassociate itself from England altogether. Nevertheless the union of England and Scotland, as Great Britain, was eventually achieved in 1707 with the Scots keeping their own legal system, law courts and Presbyterian Kirk. The union agreement brought the Scottish Parliament to an end, mainly because the Scots realised that their country could no longer prosper as a separate nation. The strength of the Westminster Parliament was increased by 16 Peers and 45 commoners, all representing Scotland.

Even after the union of the Parliaments, Scotland's problems continued. Armed attempts by the supporters of James II (Latin name, Jacobus), deposed in favour of William and Mary, led to the Jacobite Rebellions. The easily-crushed rebellion of 1715 become known as the 'Fifteen'. The 1745 rebellion resulted in a short-lived victory for 'Bonnie Prince Charlie' at Prestonpans. Following the 'Forty Five', Charlie was soundly defeated at Culloden in 1746. One result of these uprisings was that the Highland clan system was dismantled by the English, and the wearing of the tartan was forbidden.

After the Battle of Culloden, the Highlands, for the first time, came under the control of the Crown. Finding them more profitable than tenant farmers, Highland clan chiefs introduced large flocks of sheep to their lands. Many of the farmers were evicted, having become 'surplus to requirements'. The cruel and often bloody campaign, known as the 'Highland Clearances', was to be a running sore for many years.

In the light of all this it may be thought that Scotland's history is all to do with battles, castles and kings. This is not so! Scotland has had, and continues to have, its share of artists and architects, poets and pirates, not to mention scientists and engineers.

In the fifteenth century, battles or no, the poet Robert Henryson wrote his best known work, the *Testament of Cresseid,* a kind of supplement to Chaucer's *Troilus and Cressida,* and his *Robene and Makyne* is the earliest Scottish example of pastoral poetry. *Morell Fabels of Esope* is possibly his masterpiece.

John Napier, the Scottish mathematician, matriculated at St Andrew's University in 1563. He travelled on the Continent before settling down to a life of literary and scientific study. He devised many war machines, including primitive tanks; he recommended salt as a fertiliser, but he is best remembered for his prestigious inventions, logarithms and 'Napier's Bones'. Until the advent of cheap calculators in the second half of the twentieth century, multiplication and division could be simplified by the use of logarithms. Through them, multiplication was replaced by addition and division by subtraction. His 'Bones' were, in reality, a series of mechanical rods for mechanical multiplication and division. Was this the forerunner of the slide- rule?

In 1645, William Kidd was born in Greenock. In adult life he became a merchant and privateer, and his exploits as Captain Cody earned him a place in the halls of fame. He was commissioned by the Governors of New York in 1696 to suppress pirates, but succumbed to temptation and became a pirate himself. Arrested in 1699, he was sent as a prisoner to London where he was convicted of piracy and hanged.

The eighteenth century saw a veritable explosion of artistic and scientific talent. William Adam (1689 - 1748) trained his three sons Robert, James and John, as architects. The most distinguished member of the family was Robert who is considered the greatest British architect of his time and leader of the Classical revival. His work was characterised by the use of the oval, and lines of decoration in hard plaster, enlivened by painted panels in low relief. One of the greatest projects of the family was a speculatively developed district of London. It was built between Charing Cross and the River Thames and named, after them, 'the Adelphi', Greek for brothers. The area was largely demolished in 1936, but there are many surviving examples of their work both in England and Scotland.

Fourteen years after the '45 rebellion, a son was born to a small farmer in Alloway near Ayr. He later became joint tenant with his brother of the family farm, but his husbandry was lacking and the venture proved unsuccessful. His poor farming abilities were totally eclipsed by his later success as a poet. Robert Burns was to be remembered throughout the world as the national poet of Scotland. His *To A Mouse* is a prime example of Scottish verse, written in November 1785:

'Wee, sleekit, cow'rin Tim'rus beastie,
O what a panic's in thy breastie!
Thou need na start away sae hasty,
Wi bickering brattle!

> I wad be laith to rin an' chase thee
> Wi' murd'ring pattle …

He wrote many songs, one of the most famous being:

> 'O my Luve's like a red, red rose
> That's newly sprung in June
> O my Luve's like the melodie
> That's sweetly play'd in tune …

It is said that Burns' interest in women made him a kind of Scottish Don Juan. In 1786 he had 'trouble' with Jean Armour, and there was a love affair with 'Highland Mary'. He also had flirtations with 'Clarinda', among others, before returning to and marrying his old love, Jean Armour, in 1788. His birthday, 25 January, is remembered at Burns Night Celebrations in Scotland and by Scots throughout the world.

Mary Somerville was born in Jedburgh in 1780, daughter of Admiral Sir William Fairfax. She lived in London from 1816 where she moved in intellectual and scientific circles. In 1831 she published *The Mechanism of the Heavens*, a pop translation of Laplace's treatise on celestial mechanics. This had great success and encouraged her to write several more textbooks. She supported the emancipation and education of women. Somerville College, Oxford, is named after her.

Over the years, the Scots have developed a reputation for their Engineering prowess, never more so than during the Industrial Revolution which spanned the years 1750 - 1850. James Watt (1736 - 1819) developed the steam engine. He made Newcomen's steam engine vastly more efficient by cooling the used steam in a condenser separate from the main cylinder. His steam engines incorporating governors, sun-and-planet gears, and other devices were vital to the Industrial Revolution. The 'Watt', a unit of power, takes its name from him and is used to this day.

Thomas Telford is synonymous with Civil Engineering. He was responsible for the construction of many aqueducts and canals, including the Caledonian completed in 1823, and the erection of the remarkable 177 metre-span wrought-iron Menai suspension bridge completed in 1826. In Scotland he constructed over 1,600 kilometres of road and over 1,200 bridges, besides churches, manses and harbours.

John Rennie was born in Scotland in 1761 and, after working with the famous firm of Boulton and Watt, he set up as an Engineer in London in 1791. He soon became famous as a bridge builder; working in Boston, Galloway, Kelso, Leeds, Musselborough, Newton Stewart and on the old

Southwark and Waterloo Bridges. He also planned London Bridge. It was completed by his son John. He made many canals, drained fens, designed the London docks and many others. His son George also followed in his father's footsteps and became superintendent of the Mint. With his brother John, he was involved in immense engineering business projects; shipbuilding, railways, bridges, harbours, docks, machinery and marine engines. He built the first screw vessel for the Royal Navy, the Dwarf.

Towards the end of the Industrial Revolution, David Hill, a photographer, painter and pioneer in the use of the calotype process in photographic portraiture was commissioned to photograph the founders of the Free Church of Scotland. He, with fellow Scot Robert Adamson, used the calotype process of making photographic prints on silver chloride paper, newly invented by Fox Talbot. In the five years from 1843, Hill and Adamson produced over 2,500 calotypes, mostly portraits, but also landscapes.

The end of the Industrial Revolution did not subdue the seemingly endless talent of the Scots. John Logie Baird, born in 1888, pioneered television giving his first public demonstration in 1925. James Barrie wrote the children's fantasy *Peter Pan* in 1904. Alexander Graham Bell patented the telephone in 1876. Alexander Fleming, born 1881, discovered the antibiotic penicillin in 1928. Kenneth Grahame completed his masterpiece *The Wind in the Willows* in 1908. Charles Rennie Mackintosh (1868 - 1928) was an architect, designer and painter who exercised considerable influence on European design. Sadly, he was ahead of his time and is only now being appreciated.

To this day, Scottish people play a leading part in the social, economic and technical aspects of life in their own country and the United Kingdom as a whole.

Scotland's main industries have become electronics, marine engines, oil, natural gas, chemicals, textiles, clothing, printing, paper manufacture, food processing and, of course, the 'water of life' — whisky.

Scotland has had a tempestuous past, but nowadays its hills and glens are noble and at peace evoking thoughts of Hogmanay and Haggis, Monros and midges, water and whisky, and attracting visitors time and time again. But it seems that many English people do not appreciate that the life and culture of Scotland is different from that of England. Indeed, as Englishmen, we believe that the Scots have retained a social and civic pride now lost in England.

The Monarchs of Scotland

By AD 600, the many tribes north of the Clyde-Forth line, each with its own Chief, had united to form two distinct Kingdoms. The largest, Pictavia, was the land of the Picts, whilst to the west lay the Kingdom of the Scots, Dalriada. South of the line were the Strathclyde Britons and the Kingdom of Bernicia (Lothian).

In 843, Kenneth MacAlpin, King of Scots, inherited Pictavia through his grandmother, a Pictavian princess. This united the lands north of the Clyde-Forth and together they became known as the Kingdom of Alban, thus beginning the unification of Scotland. It wasn't until the late ninth century that the Strathclyde Britons were included in the unification, when Donald II installed his family as Kings of the Strathclyde Britons. Bernicia followed later in the early thirteenth century, under the rule of Alexander II.

From early in the tenth century the Scottish Royal Family appears to have developed a subtle means of succession, by passing the kingship back and forth between the two main branches of the family (descendants of both Kenneth I and Donald I). Those not in office were installed in the sub-kingdom of Strathclyde. This worked well until the end of the tenth century, when attempts by Kenneth II to establish a more lineal pattern of succession resulted in warfare. The feuds led to the loss of many lives.

It was during the reign of Alexander II that the Kingdom of Scotland, as we know it today, was finally established. Scottish rule of the Islands was restored on the marriage of James III in 1469.

Alpin, King of Dalriada (Died c.837).
|
Kenneth I (MacAlpin) (841 - 858).
First King of the Scots and Picts from 843.
|
Donald I (858 - 862).
Brother of Kenneth I.
Possibly assassinated.
|
Constantine I (862 -877).
Son of Kenneth MacAlpin.

|

Aedh (877 - 878).
Younger Son of Kenneth I.

|

Eocha and Giric I (878 -889).
Eocha, Grandson of Kenneth MacAlpin. Giric I descended from
Donald I.
Both deposed from throne in 889.

|

Donald II (889 - 900).
Son of Constantine I.

|

Constantine II (900 - 943.)
Descendant of Aedh. Abdicated to become Abbot of St Andrews.

|

Malcolm I (943 - 954).
Descendant of Donald II.

|

Indulf (954 - 962).
Son of Constantine II. Abdicated.
Ruled Sub-kingdom of Strathclyde before being elevated to King of
Scotland.

|

Dhubh (Duff) (962 - 966).
A son of Malcolm I.

|

Cuilean (Colin) (966 - 971).
Son of Indulf.
Overthrew Dhubh, possibly due to exclusion from Strathclyde
Kingdom.

|

Kenneth II (971 - 995).
Brother of Dhubh. Second Son of Malcolm I.

|

Constantine III (995 - 997).
Descendant of Cuilean, possibly Son. Murdered.

|

Kenneth III (997 - 1005).
Giric II, Son and Co-ruler. Killed in battle by Malcolm II.
|
Malcolm II (1005 - 1034).
Son of Kenneth II.
|
Duncan I (1034 - 1040).
Grandson of Malcolm II. Murdered by Cousin Macbeth (Malbeatha).
|
Macbeth (1040 - 1057).
Grandson of Malcolm II.
Killed by Malcolm III at Lumphanan.
|
Lulach (1057 - 1058).
Stepson of Macbeth.
Killed in ambush by Malcolm III, ending feud for Scottish Kingdom.
|
Malcolm III 'Canmore' (1058 - 1093).
'Canmore' = Big Head. Son of Duncan I.
|
Donald III 'Donald Bane' (1093 - 1094 & 1094 - 1097).
Son of Duncan I.
Opposed and twice deposed by two Sons of Malcolm III (nephews).
|
Duncan II (1094).
Son of Malcolm II and Ingibjorg. Killed by Uncle (Donald Bane).
|
Edgar (1097 - 1107).
Unmarried Son of Malcolm III and Margaret.
|
Alexander I 'The Fierce' (1107 - 1124).
Brother of Edgar.
|
David I (1124 - 1153).
Called 'The Saint' because of his enhancement of the Monarch's
prestige and for establishing a clear divide between England and
Scotland.

Brother of Alexander I.

|

Malcolm IV 'The Maiden' (1153 - 1165).
Called 'The Maiden' because he was so young (b. 1141),
and had a reputation for chastity.
Grandson of David I.

|

William I 'The Lion' (1165 - 1214).
Younger Brother of Malcolm IV.
Ruled 49 years –– the longest reign of any Scottish King.

|

Alexander II (1214 - 1249).
Son of William I.
Established today's Anglo-Scottish Border c. 1237.

|

Alexander III (1249 - 1286).
Son of Alexander II and Marie de Coucy.
First sovereign of whole mainland Scotland as it is today.

|

Margaret 'The Maid of Norway' (1286 - 1290) b. 1283.
Daughter of Eric II of Norway.
Granddaughter of Alexander III. Died at sea aged three years.
Last line of Malcolm II.

|

Interregnum (1290 - 1292).
Thirteen people laid claim to throne.

|

John Balliol (1292 - 1296).
Grandson of Daughter of David I. Chosen By Edward I of England.

Abdicated when Edward I invaded Scotland and declared himself
King.

|

Interregnum (1296 - 1306).
William Wallace attempted to secure independence from England,
but was executed by Edward I (known as 'The Hammer of the Scots').
Robert Bruce killed John Comyn 'The Red' and was crowned King.

|

Robert I 'Robert Bruce' (1306 - 1329).
Seized throne in 1306. Won Scotland's Independence.

|

David II (1329 - 1371).
Only surviving Son of Robert I. Succeeded father when five years old.
First anointed monarch (1331).

|

Edward Balliol (1332 - 1356).
Son of John Balliol.
Routed Scots army and forced David II into exile. Was crowned King
but, less than three months later, had to flee across Border.
Surrendered his claims to Scottish throne to Edward III of England in
1356.

|

Robert II (1371 - 1390).
Son of Walter 'The Steward' (High Steward of Scotland) and Robert
I's Daughter, Marjorie. Guardian of Scotland in David II's absence.
Founded the Stewart (later Stuart) dynasty.

|

Robert III (1390 - 1406).
Eldest Son of Robert II (was John Steward).

|

James I (1406 - 1437).
Second Son of Robert III. Uncle Robert (Duke of Albany) became
Regent whilst James spent 18 years incarcerated in Tower of London.
Was murdered at Perth.

|

James II 'The Fiery Face' (1437 - 1460).
Called 'Fiery Face' because of birthmark. Surviving twin Son
of James I. Killed by bursting cannon at Roxburgh.

|

James III (1460 - 1488).
Eldest Son of James II. Succeeded father when five years old.
On his marriage (1469), rule of Islands returned to Scotland.
Murdered by Scots rebels at Sauchieburn.

|

James IV (1488 - 1513).
Son of James III. Succeeded father when fifteen years old.
Known as the ideal medieval king. Married Margaret Tudor, eldest daughter of
Edward VII of England.

|

James V (1513 - 1542).
Succeeded Father when 17 months old.
Margaret Tudor became Regent until married in 1514, when Duke of Albany became Regent. James became independent sovereign in 1528.

|

Mary, Queen of Scots (1542 - 1567).
Also Queen of France for two years from age 16.
Daughter of James V. Succeeded Father when 7 days old.
Abdicated at insistence of Scots Lords and
executed by Cousin Elizabeth I of England in 1587.

|

James VI. (1567 - 1625)
Son of Mary, Queen of Scots and Lord Darnley (Henry Stuart).
Succeeded Mary aged one. Earl of Moray became Regent.
Became James I of England from 1603 on death of Elizabeth I.

Our present Queen is descended from a daughter (Elizabeth) of James VI (I).

Scottish Highland Welcome

Chasing a pair of rainbows down a loch
Copper-dead bracken
Living Christmas trees
Gatherings of moss
Windscreen pounded by the car-wash rain
Buds on birch
And hornbeam
Dribbling, manmade, roadside cliffs
Streams and waterfalls
Hum of side window, up
And down
Now sun, now rain
Headlights and swishing tyres

Ben Nevis

FIRST STAGE:
Fort William to Head of Loch Eil
15.5 kilometres, 9.6 miles (excluding the ferry)

If you are not being supported by a vehicle you will require provisions for five days and, of course, all the necessary lightweight camping equipment, although accommodation may be possible at the end of Stage Four.

To give this long distance walk a good start, it begins on the Fort William to Camusnagaul passenger ferry. This ferry provides a good service, Monday to Saturday only. Remember to check its timetable before planning your own.

The ferry crosses Loch Linnhe in about ten minutes and, having got

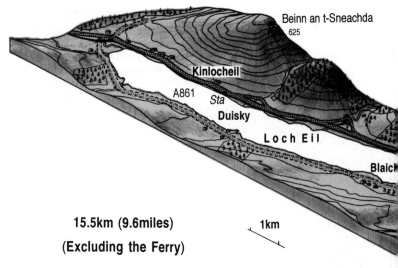

15.5km (9.6miles)

(Excluding the Ferry)

1km

a short distance away from the Fort William pier, presents you with magnificent views - visibility permitting. Ben Nevis rises beyond the town and, looking south-west from the boat, one sees Loch Linnhe disappearing into the distance, with hills rising from each side. To the north and north-east, the Great Glen lies flat and wide at its junction with the sea. Ahead, lies the little pier at Camusnagaul with trees on the lower slopes of the background hills. As you disembark, look back for one more glance at Fort William and the Ben.

Following the little-used A861 the route passes through woods to start with, but soon opens out to give views of South Morar. To the right is Loch Eil, its far foreshore dominated by the paper mill, industry and dwellings.

As these are left behind, the hills take over and you pass farms, hamlets and homes. At the head of Loch Eil, you leave the sea and join the mountains of South Morar. You won't see another metalled road until you get to Kinloch Hourn.

The going is very easy, so it can be regarded as a warm up in preparation for the tough crossing to and through Knoydart.

FIRST STAGE

Fort William (Camusnagaul) to head of Loch Eil

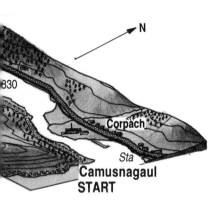

830

Corpach

Sta
Camusnagaul
START

N

There are no shops or places offering accommodation at the head of Loch Eil, but there are one or two B & Bs along the A861.

If you really do not want to walk along the A861, you could use the train and alight at Locheilside Station and then walk along the A 830 to the head of Loch Eil. However, you will lose lots of brownie points if you do!

A vehicle rendezvous is possible at the head of Loch Eil.

1.1

Navigation is so straightforward that large scale maps are unnecessary. From the centre of Fort William make your way to the loch side near the SW end of the dual carriageway (A82), where you will find a small pier. As well as accommodating the ferry, at the time of research it was occupied by a restaurant. There are several ferry crossings each day (except Sundays); their times are posted at the pier and are also available at the Tourist Information Centre.

After crossing Loch Linnhe on the ferry, you will alight at Camusnagaul. Take the A861 northwards, then westwards, on the very pleasant road walk to the head of Loch Eil. Then cross the A830 into the lane.

There are no shops, or places offering accommodation, here.

IN AND AROUND FORT WILLIAM

Gleann Mor, Glen Mor, The Great Glen and Glen Albyn are all alternative names for the major fault valley which extends across Scotland south-west from the Moray Firth to Loch Linnhe. Despite its name, Fortrose, on the Moray Firth, never did have a fort, but across the estuary lies Fort George completed by Robert Adam in 1763. Fort George was enormous, covering nearly five hectares and capable of accommodating 2,500 men. It became the depot of the Seaforth Highlanders, until they combined with the Camerons to become The Queen's Own Highlanders in 1963. At the southern end of Loch Ness, in the Great Glen, is Fort Augustus. Built as a result of the 1715 Rising, it was captured by the Highlanders in '45 and lost after Culloden. The site was presented to the Benedictine Order who built their Abbey and College there in 1876. Little of the fort remains.

Oliver Cromwell sent General George Monck to Lochaber to 'Confine the barbarism of the Highlanders'. Monck, not approving of the old Inverlochy Castle, built a fortress in 1655 on the left bank of the Nevis, where it flows into Loch Linnhe. The area was uninhabited at the time, but people in the surrounding area were naturally attracted to live by the garrison named Inverlochy. By the turn of the century Monck's fort had fallen into disrepair, but General MacKay of Scourie rebuilt and strengthened it. He renamed the fort and village Maryburgh, after the wife of newly-crowned William of Orange. It remained thus until the nineteenth century, when the Duke of Gordon bought the land and renamed it Gordonburgh. This name was never approved of by the locals, nor was Duncanburgh imposed by Duncan Cameron when he bought the estate. The fort dominated the lives of the villagers, who preferred the name Fort William in honour of William III. Eventually the local council and, more importantly the General Post Office, acknowledged local custom and Fort William it remains to this day, often affectionately abbreviated to 'Fort Bill'. The fort itself was demolished in 1864 to make way for the railway, the behemoth which also started the demise of the Caledonian Canal.

The much older Inverlochy Castle is situated on the River Lochy. The remains of this, under restoration at the time of our research, can be seen near the Inverness road, about one kilometre north of the Bridge of Nevis. Confusingly there is a second 'Inverlochy Castle' about one and a half kilometres further north, but this is merely a modern mansion converted into an hotel. The real Castle is signposted 'Old Inverlochy Castle'. It is attributed to the Comyn Family, who first arrived in Britain with William the Conqueror. Part of the family achieved high office under the King of Scots in the twelfth century and in 1260 Sir John Comyn built a castle at Inverlochy, possibly on the site of an earlier fort. Perhaps built by the second earl, George, the existing castle, standing four-square beside the dark, fast-flowing river, has been dated to the late fifteenth century. Its curtain walls have been reduced in height to six from an original nine metres, presumably in the interests of safety. The flat ground to the south-west of the castle is the site of one of the most important battles in the military history of the Highlands. Here, the Royalist army of the great Marquess of Montrose defeated the covenanting army commanded by Campbell of Argyll in 1645.

One naturally associates Ben Nevis, at 1347 metres the highest mountain in Britain, with Fort William. But the great Ben cannot be seen from the town, as the bulk of Cow Hill, 287 metres, hides it from aspiring viewers. The Ben takes its name from the nearby River Nevis which represents the Gaelic *Nemess*, meaning 'spiteful', referring to its evil repute in local folklore. The Gaelic *Beinn* means 'mountain' as is found in many Scottish mountain names. So, Ben Nevis can be said to represent 'the spiteful mountain'. Folk etymology, however, derives the name of Ben Nevis from the Gaelic *Beinn-nimh-bhathais* which translates to 'the mountain with its brow in the clouds'. A much more lyrical description but alas, according to *Brewer's Names*, incorrect.

The mountain attracts walkers from all parts of the UK, and it is estimated that some 100,000 people visit it annually. Such is its popularity that local councillors are currently discussing whether to introduce a £1.00 fee for walkers taking part in charity events, such as the Three Peaks races. This, it is said, would help to defray the rising costs of providing car parks, toilet facilities and litter collection as well as footpath repairs. Naturally, the outdoor groups are totally opposed to this proposal as it goes against the concept of free access to the countryside. The time taken by the average walker to scale the Ben is four hours up and three hours down. It is not surprising, though, that the record breakers do the route more quickly than this. The current record from Fort William Town Park to the summit and back is 1 hour 25 minutes 34 seconds, set by Kenneth Stuart on 1 September 1984. On the same day, Pauline Haworth created a new women's record with a time of 1 hour 43 minutes 25 seconds. The full course of the bridlepath covers 22 kilometres, but distance can be saved by crossing the open hillside. The Three Peaks route from sea level at Fort William to sea level at Caernarvon via the summits of Ben Nevis, Scafell Pike and Snowdon attracts thousands of competitors each year. Not many of them get near the record time of 5 days 23 hours 37 minutes, set by Arthur Eddlestone in May 1980. Anne Sayer set the women's record of 7 days 31 minutes in September 1979. The Peaks have also, of course, been done more quickly than this, by using cars, motor cycles and even helicopters to travel between the mountains.

Clearly, race participants, charity walkers and hill walkers all derive enormous pleasure from walking on the highest mountain in Britain. But, make no mistake, this is a serious mountain. At the summit plateau it is necessary to keep a sharp look out, especially in mist. The 600 metre high towers and buttresses in the north facing cliffs are masked in winter and spring by snow cornices, which project two or three metres over the lip and can be very dangerous. The summit is a lunar landscape of boulders. On exceptional days Ireland can just be seen nearly 200 kilometres away.

The ruins on the summit are those of the old observatory, established in 1883 by meteorologist Clement Wragg. This observatory was used for pioneering work in long-range weather forecasting. It was closed down in 1904, later being used for a short time as an hotel before being left to fall into ruin.

The weather conditions on Ben Nevis are, or should be, of supreme interest to all those who venture out on its slopes. The summit is normally covered in cloud, even when everywhere else is clear. This results in an average of only two hours of bright sunshine per day, and an annual rainfall of 400 centimetres. The mean monthly temperature is just below freezing point, and snow is liable to fall on any day. Permanent winter snowfalls begin in October, but by July the summit is usually clear. In the hollows, under the steep summit cliffs, snow can accumulate year-round. It has been estimated that if the mountain were just a few hundred metres higher, a glacier would be formed. At these heights, and especially as Nevis is in the path of the North Atlantic hurricanes, wind is a force to be reckoned with. Cold temperatures can usually be coped with by those well prepared. But wind-chill can be a fatal companion, as many on Nevis have found to their cost. The summit area has an average of just over 250 gales each year, many of these reaching hurricane force. In winter, wind speeds of 150, gusting to 250 kilometres per hour, are fairly frequent. The message is clear: be prepared for anything if you venture into the high mountains.

Fort William was the first town in Britain to have its streets and houses illuminated by hydroelectricity, from the generators of the British Aluminium Company. Shortly after the First World War, the company built its huge factory at the foot of Ben Nevis, opposite Inverlochy Castle. The large pipes, prominent on the slopes above the smelter, carry water from dams many kilometres away through tunnels in the mountains, to produce hydro power for the smelter. Some consider the whole installation to be an eyesore, but the Alcan Smelting and Power Company, the present site owner, is one of the biggest employers in the town.

Growth of the forestry industry is apparent to all who visit Scotland. This has been taken advantage of in Corpach, three kilometres north-west of Fort William on the Mallaig road at Annat Point. The pulp mill, Arjo Wiggins Carbonless Paper Ltd, is one of the largest industrial developments in the Highlands, and is designed to use all the timber that can be harvested from the Scottish forests. The mill occupies 32 hectares and produces pulp and paper in a continuous process. Opened in 1966, it is of modern design. The dimensions of the factory are gargantuan: the pulp mill measures 122 metres in length, the paper mill 165 metres, the finishing house 162 metres, with a power house tower 51 metres high at the end. The pulp mill was closed down in 1980; the timber being exported to Scandinavia for pulping and then returned to Corpach to be processed into paper. An incredible situation you may think, but such is the influence of economics. Another eyesore perhaps, but as you walk alongside Loch Eil on the first stage of your journey the mill will be seen to pale into insignificance against the all dominating Ben Nevis.

Today, Fort William is a bustling centre with an attractive pedestrianised High Street affording ample shopping, banking, food, restaurants, accommodation and leisure facilities. The Tourist Information Centre is situated centrally and the world-famous steam train has regular departures from Fort William to Mallaig along the celebrated West Highland Railway. The West Highland Museum houses many fascinating artifacts including relics of Jacobite times, notably the 'secret portrait' of Bonnie Prince

Charlie. This curio looks rather like a painter's palette with an apparently random design of daubs of paint. But when a metal cylinder is placed against it, the multicoloured streaks reflect on its curved surface as a miniature portrait of the famous prince.

Enjoy Fort William to the full. Enjoy the restaurants. Enjoy the pubs. Enjoy the hotels and B & Bs. Tomorrow night you will probably be cooking on a stove and sleeping in a tent. And the night after. And the night after that. Your great adventure begins here. Take advantage of all the facilities. There's nothing like it until you get to Ullapool. Assuming that you decide to visit Ullapool that is.

Did Denis
And Phil

Free of duty conversation
And the politesse of trade
He walked only with the peaceful
    ones
Like Phil
Who asked few words of him
Did Denis

Unfettered, now, from Trivia-
    Domestica
He stopped haunting his own
    past,
In open spaces,
With Phil
Found freedom and contentment
Did Denis

Here, small and insignificant
Thus innocent of power
(And Mechanicals)

They covered many distances
With glowings of achievement
With every passing season,
    passing year

Wither workday worry
'Gainst the giant scales of skies?
Sang Phil

I could even perish
And the world would still wind
    on!
Chorused Denis
Feeling bold

Then they each went to their
    home
To love it all the more
Did Denis
And Phil

Gulvain

SECOND STAGE:
Head of Loch Eil to Strathan (See Variant 2)
16 kilometres, 9.9 miles

After a pleasant stroll westwards along the southern shore of Loch Eil by way of a warm-up, you now begin the tough crossing of one of Britain's remotest regions.

As you enter Gleann Fionn Lighe, to the north, the mountains close in. On your left, beyond the river, lies a vast coniferous forest. On your right, the ground rises to Beinn an t-Sneachda (625 metres). The first three kilometres on the forest road are relatively easy, if a little rough. The way is undulating with unenclosed land on each side, but the presence of the forest across the river is strong.

Beyond the bridge, which takes you over the Fionn Lighe, lies Wauchan Cottage. Isolated as it is, the occupants did not seem to us to make their living from the hills.

After Wauchan, the glen opens out exposing the southern shoulder of Gulvain straight ahead. At 962 metres it qualifies as a Munro. After a tough walk to the head of the glen, beside Allt á Choire Réidh, you climb

41

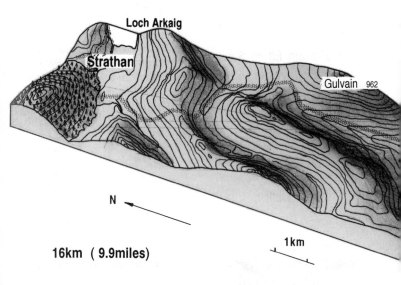

Loch Arkaig

Strathan

Gulvain 962

N

16km (9.9miles)

1km

steeply beneath the rocky outcrops of Gualann nan Osna (542 metres) reaching the bealach at about 535 metres. Pause here, perhaps for lunch as we did, and enjoy the views. Looking back to the south, the glen looks superb with its surrounding mountains. The ascent of the glen to this bealach is very steep. Indeed it could be dangerous under ice conditions, and appropriate equipment may be necessary.

The descent to Gleann Camgharaidh is also very steep, but the scenery provides an excellent reward. Again, this could be dangerous under ice conditions. However, in summer, neither the ascent nor the descent could be regarded as a scramble, as they are both on grass. Cross the river as soon as possible. Crossing higher up can be difficult for a beautiful reason: a long cascade of rushing water. The ascent out of Gleann Camgharaidh comes with glimpses of Lochan a' Chomlain reflecting the afternoon light to the south-south-west.

At the bealach, looking north, you oversee Glen Pean itself and the forest which lies between Glen Pean and Glen Dessarry. It is too easy to keep forging ahead, but we urge you to look over your left shoulder on

SECOND STAGE

Head of Loch Eil to Strathan

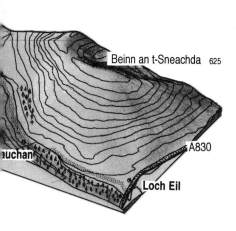

Beinn an t-Sneachda 625

A830

auchan

Loch Eil

your northerly descent to Gleann a' Chaorainn. The rocky magnificence of Streap (909 metres, not a Munro) and Streap Comhlaidh, with the corrie between them, can be truly enchanting.

After a boggy one-and-a-half kilometre walk beside the River Pean, you will find that Strathan is no more than a cottage with outbuildings; possibly used as a holiday home. Camp where you can.

A public road exists beside Loch Arkaig and gets to within two kilometres of Strathan. Be warned, however, it is narrow with passing places and it is 23 kilometres or so to the main road, so vehicular support may be problematic.

2.1 (see map p44)

A. Opposite the junction of the A861 with the A830, take the lane which gives access to the cottage. Turn right and cross the bridge over the Fionn Lighe.
B. Turn left and follow the track (forest road).
CDE. Keep on the track, passing Wauchan cottage.
F. The track changes to a well defined path.
G. Cross the bridge over the Allt á Choire Reidh. After 50 metres or so, turn left on the faint path. Do NOT proceed ahead on the defined path.
H. Ascend the glen (N), keeping more or less to the burn side. Path visible in places, but don't try to find it. Make your own way.

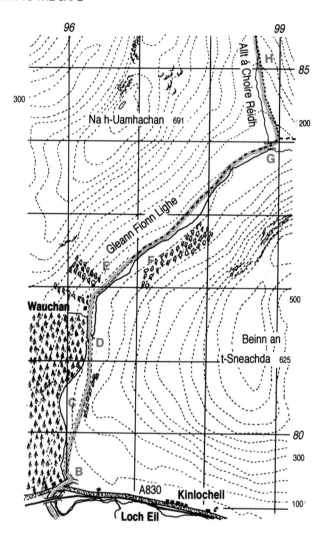

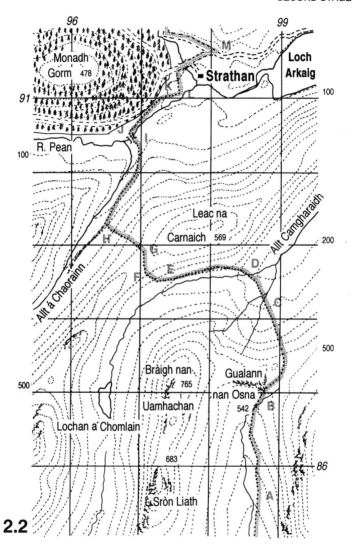

2.2

45

2.2 (see map p45)

A.   Continue ascending the glen.

B.   Turn NE. It may be advantageous to cross the burn, but make your own way to the bealach.

C.   Descend NNW to the Allt Camgharaidh. Rough going with no path.

D.   At the burn, at a point identified by a tree on a rock, turn left (W) to ascend Gleann Camgharaidh. Cross the burn when you can. No path.

E.   After about 1 kilometre, turn NW to ascend the side of the glen.

F.   You should encounter the remains of a fence (iron posts), running roughly SW to NE. Follow this line NE to the bealach at:

G.   Descend NW. Steep with no path.

H.   Join the path and descend beside the Allt á Chaorainn. Rough going.

I.   At the River Pean, cross the bridge.

J.   Turn right. No proper path. Do NOT enter the forest by the inviting stiles.

K.   Rough and wet. No path.

L.   Turn N, with the forest fence on your left, to reach the bridge over the River Dessarry. Cross, and follow the track to the junction.

M.   Turn left to ascend Glen Dessarry.

Variant 2: **Glenfinnan to Strathan**
14.5 kilometres, 9 miles
OS Landranger 40. Loch Shiel

This route is advantageous if you are short of time, wish to use hotels or B & Bs to maximum advantage, or simply hate road walking. Walk from Camusnagaul to the head of Loch Eil on the A861, as the definitive route in Stage 1. Turn left on the A830 and walk to Glenfinnan. Or, simply take the train from Fort William to Glenfinnan where there is an hotel and at least one B & B. To use the variant from the train, walk from the station at Glenfinnan for about 0.5 kilometre back along the A830 towards Fort William and at —

906808   turn left into the track leaving the A830. At —

910813   where the track crosses the River Finnan, keep ahead on the west bank of the river to pass under the railway. Continue on the defined path/track northwards to Corryhully. At —

913844	keep to the west side of the river, but turn NE. At —
920855	you MUST keep NE. OS shows no path beyond here, but we recall the semblance of one. Ascend the glen to the bealach at —
942868	continue NE, now descending into Gleann a' Chaorainn. At —
968895	join the definitive route to Strathan.

MIDGES, CLEGS, TICKS AND FLIES

During this walk, you will see majestic mountains, harmonious hills, graceful glens, raging rivers and streams serene. This unparalleled beauty will gladden your heart and uplift your soul, unless you encounter the dreaded Scottish midge. Whilst midges exist in many parts of the UK, people who have met with this particular species of Scottish fauna will confirm that it can be an unpleasant experience. How such small insects can cause so much irritation is beyond comprehension. They have become part of the mythology of walking in Scotland, and yet they are really only a problem in July and August.

Not all midges bite, but the females of some species do so ferociously. Although tiny, with a wing span of less than one millimetre, they can make dusk and dawn, not to mention a hot summer day under the trees or by the water, a real misery. These midges which feed on humans should not be confused with the dancing swarms of gnats, which rise and fall on the evening air merely trying to attract mates. Gnat swarms nearly always appear when there is a definite, although very light wind and they often keep station above conspicuous trees, bushes or other high markers.

Do not think that you can escape the Scottish midge; you cannot. You may be walking through an apparently midge-free area, decide to take a rest to enjoy the peace and tranquillity, seat yourself and get comfortable. Then, as if driven by an invisible authority, a million midges will land on your exposed flesh and tuck in to a meal of human blood. Brush them off; thousands more take their place. Try moving left or right; they will follow. Try covering all exposed parts; they will get inside the cover, any cover. The bites are not serious, but the constant irritation is quite exasperating. There seems to be only one way to escape from the slow torture of this malignant presence and that is to stand up, carry on walking and hope to find a breeze. They vanish if the windspeed is more than 6.5 kilometres per hour.

If you are indoors in 'midge country', beware of leaving windows open and lights on. Open windows AFTER extinguishing the lights.

Some people find that midge repellents work. The question is, which one? Many repellents are based on the chemical Diethyl Toluamide (DET), which comes as a liquid or in wax sticks. The liquid version is better in some circumstances, as it can be of a higher concentration and, the higher the better might be appropriate. There are various proprietary brands available at pharmacies, but we have found most preparations ineffective for us.

Observing a few unwritten rules may allow you to escape without being attacked too severely:

- Do NOT arrive at a picturesque river bank or loch side on a still, early evening and pitch your tent under the trees by the waterside. Move at least 50 metres away from the water.

- Do NOT go for boggy, low-level walks on still muggy days.

- Smoke will get rid of midges. So a campfire may be a good idea, but please observe the rules on where not to light them.

If you do get badly bitten:

- Calm the affected area by splashing with cold water or wrapping in a wet cloth.

- Apply witch hazel lotion

- In bad cases, apply anti-histamine cream.

The cleg, a type of horsefly, is a very different beast altogether. It has dull ash-grey or brown speckled wings, which it folds roof-like over its back. Clegs have brilliantly coloured, banded eyes, commonly green, gold and red. They are about one centimetre long from the biting end to the tail end, and usually attack from the waist downwards. That is not all. There is another type of horsefly (called a deerfly in America), with boldly banded wings and brilliantly spotted eyes. These flies usually bite the upper arms and head. Both are particularly nasty in that they inject the unfortunate human with an anti-coagulant, in order to ensure a steady flow of blood. They can operate through light clothing. The clegs are not as numerous as the midges, by any means, but they can still be a nuisance.

Sheep ticks can be picked up anywhere, but be particularly wary in bracken in summer. If you take a rest do not sit on the grass, but insulate yourself from ticks by sitting on a rock. Ticks, about 1.5 millimetres long, lie in wait in the grass and cling on to the hair of sheep dogs or other animals or onto the clothing of humans. If they get onto your skin they 'plug' themselves in and suck your blood, quadrupling their size in a few days. If you are unlucky enough to get one (and you won't necessarily feel it), either leave it for a few days to get nice and big or use a pair of square ended tweezers to remove it. Hold the tick's body lightly in the tweezers and 'unscrew' it. Do NOT try to pull it straight off, as you will leave the head embedded in your skin. If that happens, panic not! Apply a little antiseptic and after a week or two you will be able to pick it out. As an alternative to the tweezer method, you can apply surgical spirit or smother the tick with butter or alcohol. Don't use malt whisky; that's to be used for celebrating your victory over this voracious insect. Very easy-to-use tick removers can be bought from pharmacies in Scotland and, maybe, elsewhere.

In some areas of Scotland, a tick-borne health risk, Lymes Disease, can have serious consequences. SOME ticks, hosting on deer, carry this infection which, if transmitted to humans, can produce flu-like symptoms which lead to widespread arthritis and rheumatism. Its arrival is indicated by a spreading inflammation at the site of penetration. A quick course of antibiotics is usually enough to knock it on the head.

On a warm summer day the forests will be filled with sound. An all-pervading hum (not to be confused with the distant hum of chain-saws) is produced by countless flies, including headflies which are similar to houseflies. Whilst the swarms which surround you are annoying, they do not bite. It is the midges, clegs and ticks you should be on the lookout for.

Having warned you about the 'nasties', it must be said that there are many other varieties of fauna which serve only to enhance your enjoyment, and will cause you no problems whatsoever.

Sourlies

THIRD STAGE:
Strathan to Grid Reference 884976 (River Carnach)
17 kilometres, 10.5 miles

This stage takes you into the depths of Knoydart where the scenery is magnificent and people are few, even in the summer season.

On leaving Strathan, the entrance to Glen Dessarry is quite narrow. There is a forest of conifers across the River Dessarry on your left and the southern spur of Fraoch Bheinn (858 metres) rises steeply on your right. As you ascend, you will pass Glendessarry, which is well kept and occupied. After another one-and-a-half kilometres you pass Upper Glendessarry, a cottage which also was occupied when we did the journey.

After Upper Glendessarry the track becomes a well-defined path and follows the edge of another forest for quite a way, so the sense of isolation is not yet upon you. Definition of the path deteriorates towards the head of the glen as the mountains close in. To the north are three Munros and a Top, all craggy monsters: Sgurr na Ciche (1040 metres), Garbh Chioch Mhor (1013 metres), Sgurr nan Coireachan (953 metres) and Gorbh Chioch Bheag (968 metres) respectively.

At the bealach there are the remains of an iron gate which, presumably, once marked the boundary between two estates. When we were here in 1983 we clearly remember having to open the gate and close it after us, despite the doubtful effectiveness of the adjoining fences.

Just beyond the bealach you will come across Lochan a Mhàim, which in reality is two lochans joined by a narrow channel. The mountains really have you cornered here, rising sheer and close both north and south.

The descent to Loch Nevis is unsparing, undefined and steep in places. You will leave Loch a Mhàim on the south side of the river. But you must cross to the north side as soon as possible before the very steep descent, for the river tumbles down a gully which is deep and impossible to ford. Under ice conditions, this descent will certainly require appropriate equipment.

As you continue, the head of Loch Nevis comes into view, but its size cannot be appreciated until you get to Sourlies. It is a sea loch, but the open sea (however that is defined in this part of Scotland) is some 20 kilometres away.

There is no formal path beyond Sourlies, so walk along the foreshore until you reach the headland, over which you will have to scramble. Once on top, pause and look along Loch Nevis which seems to be cut off from the sea, six kilometres away, where the kyle turns behind a protruding hill.

Progress to and then beside the River Carnach is not difficult, although drainage channels across the flat strath may mean that one kilometre on the map becomes one-and-a-half on the ground as you twist and turn to cross them. You might be lucky and see deer grazing in this area. You can't miss the forlorn ruins of what must have been a croft at Carnoch, on the other side of the river.

When in spate, crossing the river can be difficult, so cross at the earliest opportunity. Camp before the glen narrows, as sites become fewer as flat areas become scarce. However, if you have the time and the inclination, you could proceed another two kilometres or so, and camp at 883993; or yet further at 890995.

There is no road access at the end of this Stage.

THIRD STAGE

Strathan to 884976

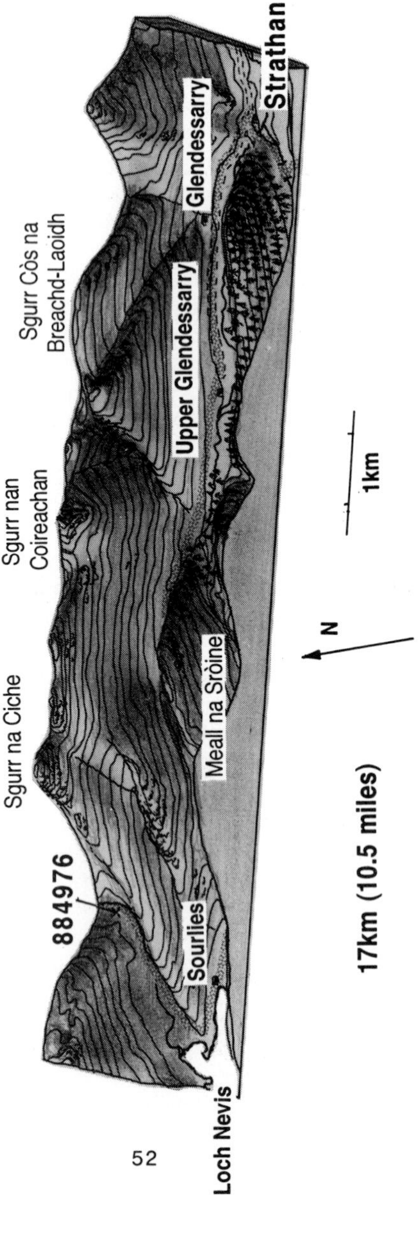

Strathan

Glendessarry

Sgurr Còs na
Breachd-Laoidh

Upper Glendessarry

Sgurr nan
Coireachan

Meall na Sròine

Sgurr na Ciche

884976

Sourlies

Loch Nevis

N

1km

17km (10.5 miles)

52

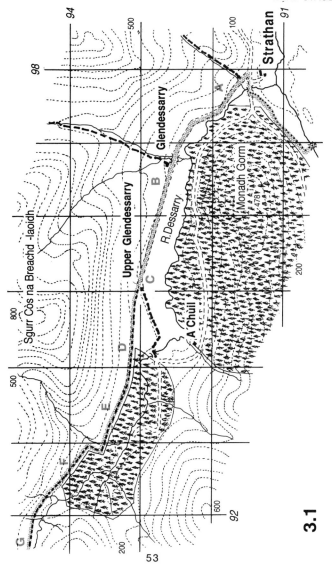

Strathan

Monadh Gorm
478

200

Glendessarry

Upper Glendessarry

R. Dessarry

A Chùil

Sgurr Còs na Breachd -laoidh

800

500

600

200

A

B

C

D

E

F

G

100

500

94

98

91

92

53

3.1

3.1 (see map p53)

A. Take the track NW to Glendessarry (Lodge).
B. Continue on the track to Upper Glendessarry (Cottage).
C. Turn right just before the 'drive' to the cottage. Ascend the path.
DEF. Continue to ascend the glen on the defined path.
G. On the approach to the bealach, the path becomes undefined.

3.2 (see map p55)

A. Cross the burn and follow the path. There are the remains of an iron gate at the summit.
B. Path not defined, but keep to the S side of the burn.
C. Keep to the S side of Lochan a Mhàim.
D. You need to cross the burn to its N side, but the formal crossing point is not easy to find. You must cross before the cascade of waterfalls, which tumble a hundred metres or so.
E. Continue the descent on the N side of the burn, then turn N at the seashore for a few metres before turning NW.
F. Pass Sourlies and on to the foreshore.
G. Keep to the foreshore as long as possible, but you will need to leave it to cross the point at:
H. Round the point, then keep level on the boggy undefined path at the foot of the steep hillside on your right.
I. You need to cross the River Carnach as soon as possible, but it is wide. At the time of research, we could not cross for about two kilometres (and only then with difficulty). (*)
J. Keep to the W side of the river.
K. We suggest that you camp near to 884976, where the ground is suitable. As you proceed N, the glen narrows and suitable sites become rare.

(*) Scottish Hill Tracks, but not OS, indicates a (foot) suspension bridge across the River Carnach near the ruins of Carnoch Village (866965). Because of necessary detours and the mistaken assumption that the river would be easy to ford further up, we did NOT investigate this bridge. You may wish to do so.

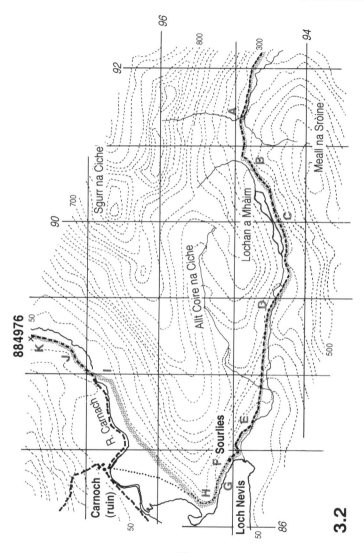

884976

3.2

In the depths of Knoydart

FOURTH STAGE:
Grid Reference 884976 to Kinloch Hourn
20 kilometres, 12.4 miles

If you are as lucky as we were, you will waken to hopes of a fine day with the tops only lightly covered in cloud. Looking north, in the direction of travel, you may feel closed in. Fear not, there is a way out, even though the glen narrows and the path is not well defined. The going is strenuous beside the river, with its small, rugged (mostly birch) trees and inaccessible crags.

As you turn north-east, you come upon a dell in which OS indicates a ruin. The setting is delightful, but isolated with a vengeance. There is no evidence of a ruin. Perhaps it was a solitary dwelling, or an outbarn, or just a simple shelter for animals?

One kilometre ahead and higher, the glen opens out and the sides are

56

less steep. Indeed, you may have chosen to camp here, as mentioned before in Stage Three. We found the spot magical and peaceful, enhanced by superb spring weather and a sprinkling of budding birch trees.

As you scramble northwards, up the glen side, you begin to see further and further, especially through a narrow gorge east-north-east. Higher still, you will look down on Lochan nam Breac and, beyond that, see the head of Loch Quoich. This area has some of the highest rainfall in the Highlands. 200 - 250 centimetres per annum is quite common, but nearer the coast this average falls markedly to 150 - 200 centimetres. The backdrop to all this is Sgurr Mór at 1003 metres.

Your route ascends north-west along a path which winds and climbs, with Luinne Bheinn left ahead at 939 metres. To your right is the shoulder of Sgurr a' Choire-bheithe. We paused at the bealach for lunch, looking ahead and down Gleann Unndalain.

The descent of the glen is straightforward, on a defined path. Lower down, the outer reach of Loch Hourn appears with the twin peaks of Druim Fada above and beyond the far shore, near sea level, the ground is flat. There are houses and a working farm at Barrisdale, where there is a track,

FOURTH STAGE

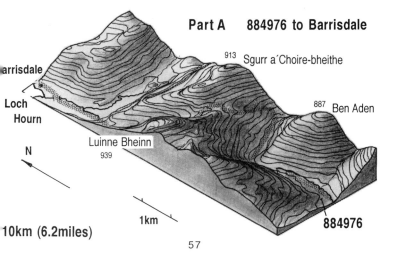

Part A   884976 to Barrisdale

913 Sgurr a´Choire-bheithe

887 Ben Aden

arrisdale

Loch Hourn

N

Luinne Bheinn
939

1km

884976

10km (6.2miles)

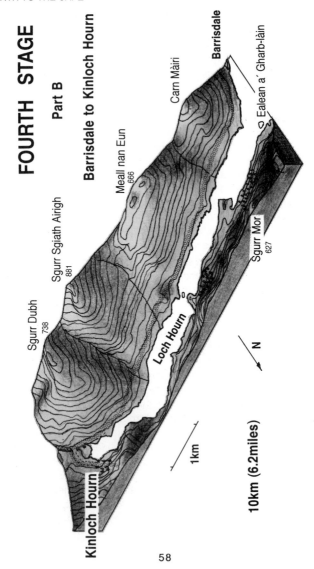

FOURTH STAGE

Part B

Barrisdale to Kinloch Hourn

Sgurr Dubh
738

Sgurr Sgiath Airigh
881

Meall nan Eun
666

Carn Màiri

Barrisdale

Ealean a' Gharb-làin

Sgurr Mor
627

Loch Hourn

N

Kinloch Hourn

1km

10km (6.2miles)

about three kilometres long, linking the dwellings and carrying farm traffic. There is no overland route from main roads for these agricultural vehicles, so they must have been brought in by sea. The postman sails from Coran on the north side of the loch but, while he may take passengers, his boat is probably too small for carrying vehicles. A larger boat must have been used, or perhaps the vehicles were delivered by a helicopter?

At the north end of the track you will find a small building, which appears to be associated with boating. Here, you join a path which is laborious. It winds and climbs and descends, but it brings you to the upper reach of Loch Hourn below on your left. It may look beautiful in summer, but no sun shines on this south shore for the five months of winter. On your right, the mountains rise to the order of 800 metres. By the far shore, they are beginning to lose height and gain a covering of woods. One or two houses stand by the water. They seem to be inhabited, yet only accessible by boat.

Loch Hourn, sometimes sombre even on sunny days, has been compared by some writers to a Norwegian fjord. The scale in Norway, however, is much vaster and the comparison is somewhat exaggerated.

One kilometre before reaching Kinloch Hourn, you join a metalled lane; a welcome relief after eight kilometres, or so, on the path.

Most of this stage is on defined paths, if vague in places. But, be aware that the going is arduous and consequently slow. These last eight kilometres into Kinloch Hourn seem particularly difficult. Probably because one is tired and, perhaps, footsore.

A farm at Kinloch Hourn offers limited B & B, but don't rely on its being available. It is at the head of a winding and narrow public road (a lane by our definition), which has been described as 'the most beautiful (and longest) cul-de-sac in Britain'. It runs through a deserted Glen Garry, which, before the Clearances was home to some 5,000 men, women and children. At the end of its 35 kilometres, from the A87 near Invergarry, the road descends between rocks, worn smooth by thousands of years of glacial activity, to Kinloch Hourn. No longer a thriving fishing village, it remains an isolated haven for the hillwalker, the fisherman and the resolute motor car tourist. This road can be busy, but 'busy' is, of course, a relative term. So you may be lucky with the B & B, but no provisions are available here.

4.1

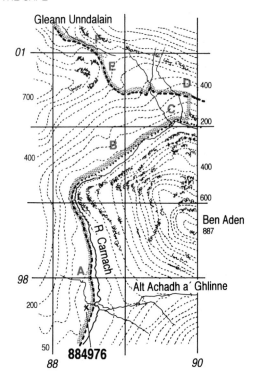

4.1

A. Keep on the W side of the River Carnach. The path is defined in places as it passes through the narrow gorge.

B. The valley is wider. The path undefined, but keep to the same side of the river.

C. At a bend where the river comes from a gorge to the SE, leave the river to ascend the very steep side of the glen (N). No path or any indication of route.

D. After ascending 100 metres, or so, a defined path is encountered. Turn left to continue the ascent, but less steeply.

E. Path defined, with many zigzags, to the bealach at:

F. Good view ahead down Gleann Unndalain to the NW. Descend.

4.2

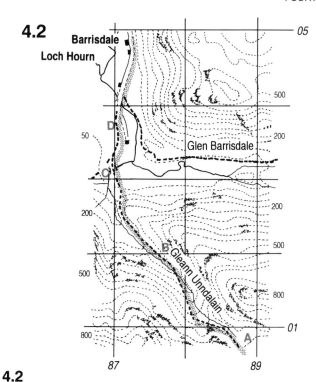

4.2

ABC. Descend on the defined path, then cross the burn via the bridge.

D. Join the track and continue N through Barrisdale.

61

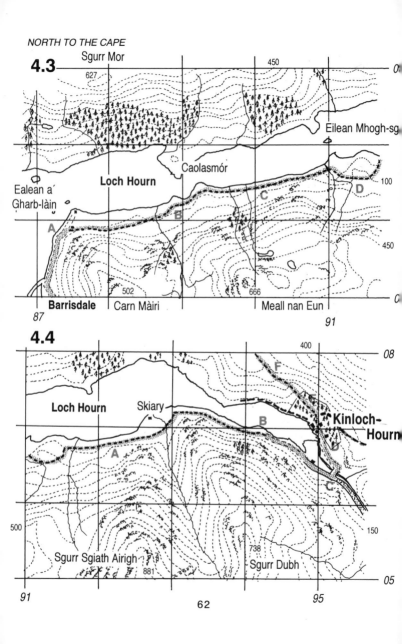

4.3

A.   Just before the ruin, leave the track to join the well-defined track/path ascending E.

BCD. Follow the path which is well defined all the way to the head of Loch Hourn. It is rough in places, ascends and descends, twists and turns and is surely longer than the 8.5 kilometres that the map indicates.

4.4

A.   Keep on the path.

B.   Join the metalled lane.

C.   Cross the bridge over the river. This gives access to Kinloch Hourn House. Continue on the track into the grounds of the house.

D.   Keep the cottages on your right and approach the house. Turn right at the house (do NOT pass in front). The path is well defined.

E.   Keep ascending on the well-maintained path. Various branches are present, but these are, presumably, the walkways of the formal gardens.

F.   On leaving the enclosed grounds the path is still well maintained. Ascend NW.

THE CALEDONIAN CANAL

During the Devonian Period of geological time, 408 - 360 million years ago, the Pre Cambrian rocks in what is now known as the Scottish Highlands suffered extensive faulting. Rocks to the north of the Great Glen Fault, the largest in the British Isles, moved about 102 kilometres to the south-west. Had the fault been only tens of metres deeper, it is estimated that it would have filled with water and that the land mass to the north would have become an island. As it was, four lochs developed in the Great Glen, all joined by rivers. This freak accident of nature was put to good use in relatively modern times, when Thomas Telford supervised the building of the world-famous Caledonian Canal. Of its 98 kilometre length, only 37 kilometres is artificial, the rest being the natural lochs: Lochy, Oich, Ness and Dochfour.

In the late eighteenth century, certain factors combined to lead the Government of the day to decide that a canal should be built between Fort William and Inverness. The main factor was that sailing ships were often taking many days to navigate the hazardous sea journey via the Minch, around Cape Wrath and through the Pentland Firth into the North Sea. Also, in Scotland at that time, considerable Government aid was available for building works. This was a political move to try and stop the emigration from the Highlands of families escaping from the warlike Jacobite uprisings. And, anyway, canal building was in vogue.

Thomas Telford (1757 - 1834) was born in Langholm, son of a shepherd. Apprenticed to a local stonemason at the age of 14, he later went to Edinburgh and then to London in 1782. Two years later he got work in Plymouth Dockyard, and in 1787 was appointed Surveyor of Public Works for Shropshire. He quickly gained a reputation as a first class civil engineer to the extent that, later in life, he became the first President of the Institution of Civil Engineers. He is now acknowledged as the father figure of the British civil engineering profession. In 1801, Telford was commissioned by the Government to report on public works required in Scotland. He was to conduct a feasibility study for a canal, and assess its value to the Navy in the wars with France. He was also to advise on whether or not a canal could be built using local effort.

Telford's recommendations were for a canal six metres deep by twelve metres wide. He estimated that it would take seven years to build, at a cost of £350,000, and that local labour supervised by experienced engineers and craftsmen could cope with the job. The necessary Acts of Parliament were passed. Commissioners were appointed to oversee the project and administer the funds of what became the first state-funded transport undertaking in the UK. Beginning work in 1803, Telford was about to verify one of Edmund Burke's many philosophical statements. Burke (1729 - 97) was of the opinion that: 'Those who carry on great public schemes must be proof against the worst delays, the most mortifying disappointments, the most shocking insults and, what is worst of all, the presumptuous judgments of the ignorant upon their designs'. Telford's skills were stretched to the limit. Difficulties escalated. Financial estimates were exceeded and completion dates eclipsed. The canal, only four and a half metres deep, was finally opened in 1822. It cost £840,000. This was not the last time a big civil engineering project has overrun in time and cost. It must be a characteristic of the profession, or a device to get a project started which cannot then be abandoned!

Meanwhile, thanks to the Industrial Revolution, sailing ships started to be replaced by steamships capable of navigating the northern coast more easily. Also, most ships were now too big to go through the canal. The French wars were over. Was this the death knell for Britain's longest short cut? Despite the plentiful protestations of critics, it was decided that the canal was too valuable to lose. In any case, it was doubtful and most improbable that the many engineering achievements could be reversed. The canal was taken out of service from 1844 to 1847 for deepening and other improvements.

Vessels enter the western terminal basin of the canal through a sea lock at Corpach. This basin was cut from solid rock by navvies using hammers, chisels, picks, shovels and explosives. A brewery was built nearby to encourage the navvies to drink beer rather than whisky. However, the brewery had the effect of enticing the navvies to drink beer AND whisky. Was this the derivation of the famous Scottish combination 'a hauf and hauf' (beer with a whisky chaser)? Despite, or because of, these bibulous difficulties, the basin was excavated, although it was smaller than desirable due to the hard rock. A pair of locks were constructed to lift vessels out of the basin and on to Banavie.

Banavie is one of the most magnificent areas of the Canal. Not only because it lies in the shadow of Ben Nevis, but also because of Neptune's Staircase. This is a spectacular staircase flight of eight locks, giving a rise of 19.5 metres. It has been described as the most remarkable series of locks in the UK. From the highest lock the canal meanders its way for several kilometres to Gairlochy where it enters Loch Lochy, with its regulating lock, built to maintain water level differentials. But, when this lock was swamped in 1834, a second one, supplemented by further flood barriers, was built. As with all the lochs, miniature lighthouses stand sentinel at each end of Loch Lochy to mark the entrances to the canal sections.

The exit from Loch Lochy is by the staircase pair of Laggan Locks. Laggan is the site of a bloodbath. This terrible fight between the clans MacDonald and Fraser took place in 1544. It was July. The weather was very hot and the men removed their shirts before engaging in a ferocious battle, known as The Battle of the Shirts. Only a handful survived the carnage.

East of Laggan Locks, the canal passes through the long, tree-lined Laggan Cutting. This, one of Telford's least known but most impressive works, leads vessels to the summit, Loch Oich.

Careful account of water supplies is usually paramount when designing canal systems. Not so with the Caledonian. Surrounded by unsurpassed mountain scenery, Loch Oich, the shallowest of the four lochs and 34 metres above sea level, supplies limitless water in both directions. Two single locks lead out of this loch and through five secret kilometres to a staircase of five locks into Loch Ness, surely the most famous loch of all. It is world famous for its size, its rugged grandeur and, of course, for its monster. It is a fresh water loch 15 metres above sea level. It is deeper than the North Sea, 213 metres for much of its length and even 274 metres in places. It is 39 kilometres long and up to 2.5 kilometres wide, with a surface area of 91 square kilometres. The estimated volume of water, which never freezes, is 7,450,000,000 cubic metres, making it the largest body of fresh water in the British Isles; larger than all the lakes and reservoirs of England and Wales combined.

The famous, or infamous, monster is not a new discovery. Legend has it that Saint Columba banished an 'aquatilis bestie' from the waters in the sixth century. There have been thousands of claimed sightings over the years, but there is little actual evidence. In 1968 and 1975, the Loch Ness Investigation Bureau collaborated with scientific teams and conducted sonar tests. The first series of tests revealed the presence of 'large animate objects'. The second series appeared to confirm the existence of a monster, but the findings of all the tests were later rejected. Is there a monster? You will have to make up your own mind about this 'fresh water Leviathan'. One thing for sure is that 'Nessie' attracts would-be viewers year after year.

From Loch Ness, a narrow stretch of water connects with the smallest of the four lochs, Loch Dochfour, at the exit of which a single regulating lock takes vessels into a canal section to the outskirts of Inverness. A staircase of four locks at Muirtown leads out into the Beauly Firth at Clachnaharry.

Telford's masterpiece was never commercially successful, mainly because the size of the newly introduced steamships quickly outgrew the lock dimensions. By their very nature the works of civil engineers usually stand the test of time, remaining as fine monuments to their creators' capabilities. The Caledonian Canal, still used to this day, will remain for many years a very visible and very beautiful memorial to that master engineer Thomas Telford. The administrative headquarters of the waterway is situated at Clachnaharry. On one of the office walls is inscribed a poem written by Robert Southey, in which he praises the work of Telford:

> Telford it was by whose presiding mind
> The whole great work was planned and perfected...
> Telford who o'er the vale of Cambrian Dee
> Aloft in air at giddy height upborne
> Carried with navigable road; and hung
> High o'er Menai's Strait the bending bridge:
> Nor hath he for his native land performed
> Less in this proud design: and where his piers
> Around her coast from many a fisher's creek
> Unsheltered else, and many an ample port
> Repel the assailing storm: and where his roads
> In beautiful and sinuous line far seen
> Wind with the vale and win the long ascent
> Now o'er the deep morass sustained, and now
> Across ravine, or glen or estuary
> Opening a passage through the wilds subdued.

The Saddle

FIFTH STAGE:
Kinloch Hourn to Shiel Bridge (See Variant 5)
15.5 kilometres, 9.6 miles

Kinloch Hourn on a fine spring morning is enchanting. The clarity of light is unforgettable and seems unique to these northern latitudes. Maybe there is little dust in the air because of its great distance from human activity, or perhaps the reflections from numberless particles of dew give the light its sparkling quality: "Oh to be in Kinloch Hourn now that April's there" (with apologies to Robert Browning).

The big house overlooks the northern tip of the loch head. Behind, the house is protected by woodland presumably planted by a previous owner as part of the ornamental garden. Indeed, as you pass through the grounds, you could easily take a wrong turning and find yourself on a tour of the estate.

You will leave the formal gardens through a gate and ascend on a well-engineered path. As you get higher, look back across the treetops at the green farmland, the river, and the road which disappears around a shoulder then climbs on up and over to Loch Quoich. Higher still, look south and south-west over Loch Hourn. Seek out the far shore and the scenic, if tortuous, path you travelled on yesterday. In good weather you

68

will find it difficult to drag yourself away to continue the climb.

The intimate feel of the first kilometre, or so, is lost about three kilometres from Kinloch Hourn, as the landscape opens out to a vast amphitheatre. But the going is easy on a defined path, just off which you will encounter an estate shelter where you can rest and reflect.

The next section is a bit of a trudge, but the glen narrows as one ascends and becomes more interesting. The climb to the lochan at the bealach under Forcan Ridge is steep, but hardly a scramble (take great care, though, in icy conditions). Behind you is Loch Hourn; ahead and down, Glen Shiel. Tempting as it looks, you do not go down to Glen Shiel (unless you want to get off the mountain, fast), but turn left, and north, to make for a long line of large stones which seem to guard a very rough and slow path. Which came first, the path or the stones, we know not. Nor have we attempted to throw light on the genesis and purpose of the stones, but they provide a welcome navigation guide for travellers like us passing under the Forcan Ridge. You may be lucky, as we were, and see ptarmigan in this area. Also known as the white grouse, or rock grouse, its grey and black plumage, which changes to white in the winter, provides a very effective camouflage when in its habitat of grey and black rocks.

From the summit of Meallan Odhar, there are good views of Glen Shiel, east, north-east and north. Westward is the massif of The Saddle (1010 metres). Its summit, truly a saddle slung between two peaks of equal height, looks especially grand when patched with snow.

The descent into the glen of the River Allt a' Choire Choil is steep, but not difficult. It is followed by a plod beside the river all the way to Shiel Bridge. However, less than a kilometre before the village, the river, now called Allt Undalain, breaks through a rocky barrier in a beautiful gorge and then cascades down to join the River Shiel.

There are two old bridges and you cross them both. The second, and larger of the two, is the original Shiel Bridge. This should not be confused with the Shiel bridge on Loch Shiel or, indeed, the Bridge of Shiel which is about eight kilometres to the SE on the A87. The Bridge of Shiel was the site of a little known Jacobite confrontation, involving thousands of men, including several hundred Spaniards, in 1719.

A camping and caravan site is on your right as you approach the first bridge, and another at nearby Morvich (See next Stage). There is also a Youth Hostel at Ratagen on the south-west shore of Loch Duich, two kilometres away. Hotel and B & B accommodation is available in Shiel Bridge and the petrol station shop is well stocked. A Tourist Information Centre is situated outside the hotel, but is not open all year

FIFTH STAGE

Kinloch Hourn to Shiel Bridge

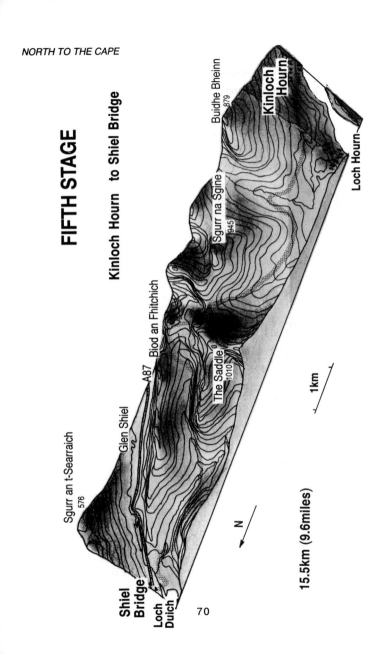

Sgurr an t-Searraich
576

Glen Shiel

A87

Biod an Fhitchich

Buidhe Bheinn
879

Sgurr na Sgine
945

The Saddle
1010

Kinloch Hourn

Loch Hourn

Shiel Bridge

Loch Duich

N

1km

15.5km (9.6miles)

5.1 **A.**   After a short descent, the path bifurcates. Keep right.

    B. Keep right on the well-engineered path, NE.

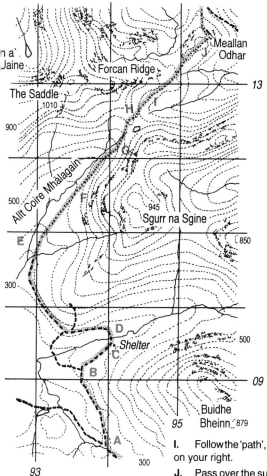

C.   Just off the path, before the crossing of the burn, an estate shelter is available for use. On p73 (*) is a reproduction of the notice therein. Your sense of responsibility will cause you to adhere to the requests.

D.   Cross the burn and follow the path.

E.   At the Allt Coire Mhàlagain, the path stops. From here there is no formal path. We suggest that you keep ascending NE on the E side of the burn.

F.   Find your own route. The going is not difficult, but very rough and slow. Do not rush.

G.   Steep ascent. No path.

H.   At the beal-ach, keep to the left (north side) of the lochan. Turn left, keep on the contour and make for the line of large stones 200 metres NNE. This line is the course of a very rough path.

I.   Follow the 'path', keeping the large stones on your right.

J.   Pass over the summit of Meallan Odhar.

71

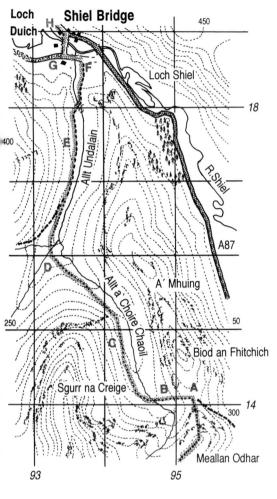

5.2

A. From the bealach, Glen Shiel is far down on your right. If you want a quick descent, turn right and follow the well-defined path down to the A87. If you do this, you will have a long march down the road to Shiel Bridge.

B. Descend to the Allt à Choire Chaoil and cross it as soon as possible. (A later crossing may be difficult.)

C. Descend the glen, keeping the burn on your right. No path.

D. Cross the burn and ascend to the path.

E. Follow the well-defined path to the car park.

F. At the 'old road' (the old A87?), turn left and over the bridge.

G. Turn right and over the bridge (presumably the original Shiel Bridge), to the A87.

H. Turn left at the A87 and into Shiel Bridge village.

Variant 5: **Kinloch Hourn to Shiel Bridge**
20.3 kilometres, 12.6 miles
OS Landranger 33. Loch Alsh & Glen Shiel

This route is longer then the definitive one but is probably navigationally simpler, especially under severe weather conditions. OS shows paths all the way to the A87, but the last 6.5 kilometres is a plod down Glen Shiel on this road.

Leave the bridge at Kinloch Hourn to follow the definitive route for about 0.75 kilometre, passing the big house and starting the ascent. At —

950072 a path to the right leaves the climb and keeps SE on the contour. Leave the trees and keep level, then turn NE into the glen carrying the Allt Coire Sgoireadail. At —

963071 cross the burn to join the path on the other side. Follow this path up the glen to the bealach at —

976098 Then descend into the upper reaches of Glen Quoich.

980103 Near the lowest point, turn left to join another path and ascend NW.

966114 At Bealach Duibh Leac, descend the zigzag path. Then follow the glen NNE down to the A87. At —

971140 turn left and march down the A87 to Shiel Bridge.

KINLOCH HOURN ESTATE
WE WOULD NOT MIND IF YOU USE
THIS SHED FOR A SHORT REST
BUT PLEASE DO NOT USE A
GAS STOVE OR LIGHT A FIRE
IN OR AROUND THE SHED
THANK YOU
PLEASE MAKE SURE DOOR IS PROPERLY CLOSED
WHEN YOU LEAVE

---

* Handwritten Sign at Estate Hut.

Shiel Bridge

SIXTH STAGE:
Shiel Bridge to Killilan
22.5 kilometres, 14 miles

From Shiel Bridge, you will require provisions for two days.

The first part of this stage is along roads and lanes, the distance depending upon where you stayed. If you stayed at the camping and caravan site at Morvich, you will have less than a kilometre on a lane. Whichever your starting point, you walk along the south side of Strath Croe, passing quite a few well-kept dwellings. After crossing the River Croe, you leave habitation as the path follows the course of the Abhainn Chohaig, this being on your left. On your right, the north-western flank of Beinn Bhuidhe rises steeply, with the Five Sisters of Kintail beyond it. If you are a Munro bagger, you could stay a while in the Shiel Bridge area

74

and claim the Sisters. You will, of course, already have 'done' The Saddle, and maybe others, on your way to Shiel Bridge.

You will have noticed from the OS maps of this area, the large number of so-called forests where there are no trees as such. For example, in previous stages you will have passed through the forests of Barrisdale, Kinloch Hourn and Glen Shiel, whilst in this stage you pass through Kintail Forest and Inverinate Forest. In England, forest, in this context, refers to an area originally reserved for hunting, whether there be trees or no, or to an area once covered by trees. The same applies in Scotland where there are many hectares of treeless deer forests.

As you proceed north you enter a modern forest, with trees. At the time of research there had been extensive harvesting, so there were views all around. Because of this, it would have been easy to look forward and make the wrong assumption about which glen the route enters. Never neglect details in navigation. The route through this modern forest is pleasant enough, taking the forest roads.

Once clear of the forest, there is a steady climb in the open, albeit up a narrow glen, to Bealach na Sròine from which there are fine panoramas

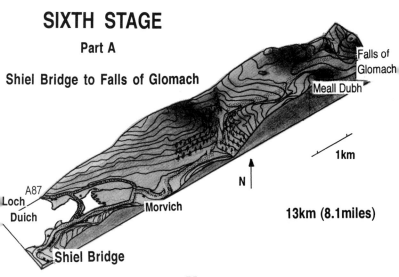

SIXTH STAGE

Part A

Shiel Bridge to Falls of Glomach

Falls of Glomach

Meall Dubh

1km

N

A87

Loch
Duich

Morvich

13km (8.1miles)

Shiel Bridge

SIXTH STAGE

Part B

Falls of Glomach to Killilan

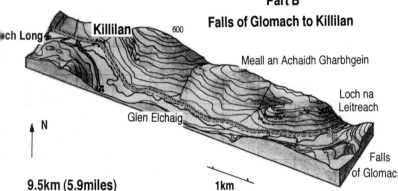

9.5km (5.9miles)

ahead (north-east) and behind.

The descent to the Falls of Glomach (the hidden falls) is straightforward and open. The falls are spectacular. The river tumbles 150 metres or so into a ravine (clough in Scotland) in one large leap of just over 100 metres, followed by a cascade of smaller ones. This is not, as is often supposed, the largest waterfall in Britain, but it has one of the biggest single leaps and is the most impressive of all.

The path leads naturally to a viewpoint, but it is steep and can be dangerous. Do take care. We recommend that you do not attempt the descent to the viewpoint, short as it is, in conditions of wet weather, ice and snow.

From here, you will have to climb back to the main path, before continuing your journey. This path, too, despite being reasonably well defined, could be quite dangerous, for it hangs on the west side of the gorge. Even in perfect walking conditions, one must take care. In poor visibility, proceed very slowly and follow the path step by step. In conditions of snow or ice, we recommend the use of appropriate equipment. The way down gradually becomes less treacherous, but care is still needed.

After crossing the Allt a' Ghlomaich on the footbridge, there are no ground problems, even in winter. A short walk brings you to the River Elchaig and its twin bridges, then onto the track along Glen Elchaig.

76

It is a long march down the glen to Killilan, the track becoming a lane in due course. But, there are compensations: the scenery is good; a large herd of Highland cattle should provide a spree for animal photographers; the glen is littered with glacial erratics, something we had not seen on our research so far on this trip.

Killilan is a very tidy hamlet. There is a very large, disused building near the houses in Killilan which looks as if it was once an hotel or shooting lodge. What a shame it is not an hotel now, for there are no facilities here whatsoever (apart from a telephone). It is obviously a working community, so do be discreet on your choice of campsite. There is no public access for vehicles, although if you are being supported by a vehicle, a rendezvous at the car park a kilometre or so down the road would be practical.

6.1

A. Fork right, to leave the main road and take the lane to Ault a' chruinn and Carn-gorm.

B. Turn right on the lane to Morvich. Keep the caravan

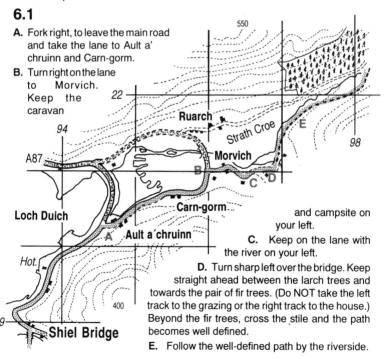

and campsite on your left.

C. Keep on the lane with the river on your left.

D. Turn sharp left over the bridge. Keep straight ahead between the larch trees and towards the pair of fir trees. (Do NOT take the left track to the grazing or the right track to the house.) Beyond the fir trees, cross the stile and the path becomes well defined.

E. Follow the well-defined path by the riverside.

6.2

A.   Fork left to descend to the river and the bridge crossing.

B.   Ascend to the forest road and turn right. Follow the road.

C.   Keep on the forest road and cross the burn. The various roads may be confusing, but, after the burn crossing, you must proceed northwards on the E side of the burn.

D.   Cross the burn on the bridge to leave the forest area. Ascend steeply for a few metres, then turn right. Path well defined.

EFG.   Ascend to Bealach na Sròine and descend. Path well defined.

H.   Turn NW and the Falls of Glomach are on your right. The path directs you to the viewpoint. There are signs warning of danger. Take great care!

I.   Retreat from the viewpoint and find the path, which is not clear at first but it ascends NW under the cliff.

J.   Path well defined, but precarious. Take great care, as a slip may mean not just a broken leg but a fall of a hundred metres or so into the ravine. Only attempt this route in snow/ice conditions if you have the necessary experience and equipment.

K.   Descend steeply. Path defined and less precarious. At the foot of the descent, the burn may be difficult to cross when in spate.

L.   Keep on the SW side of the burn, on the defined track.

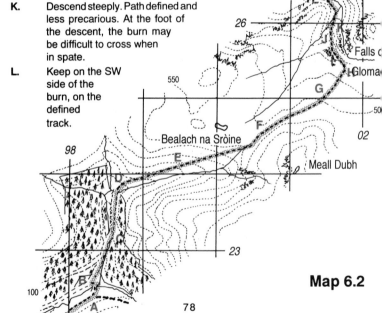

Map 6.2

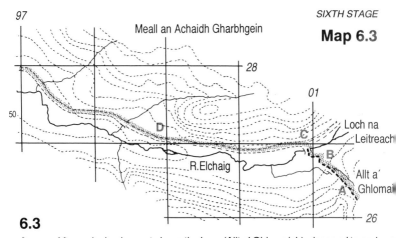

Map 6.3

6.3

A. After a slushy descent above the burn (Allt a' Ghlomaich), descend to and cross the footbridge.

B. The path leaves the burn where it bends SW. Proceed E of N, then turn left (W) to follow the river to the double footbridge.

C. Cross the bridges and ascend to the track. Turn left (SW).

D. Continue on the track.

THE BAGPIPES

Scotland means different things to different people. Some will associate it with whisky. Others will think first of haggis. Tartan will evoke thoughts of Scotland in most of us. But it is probably the bagpipe which is universally synonymous with that fair country, north of the Border.

Curiously, the origins of this ancient instrument do not lie in Scotland. Mentioned in the Bible, it dates back at least a thousand years before Christ. The ancient Greeks played the bagpipe, and its use by Roman armies led to it reaching Britain. Known throughout Europe in medieval times, it is still played in parts of Eastern Europe, Ireland and, of course, Scotland.

Over the centuries, details have changed but the fundamental principle of its construction and the manner of playing have remained more or less constant. It has a leather wind-bag, serving the same purpose as the wind-chest of an organ, which the player fills with air by blowing through

Map 6.4

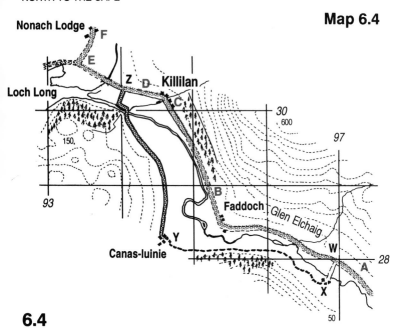

6.4

ABC. Continue on the track, which becomes a lane, all the way to Killilan. The eight kilometres of track/lane is an estate road, along which only estate vehicles are permitted, so if you are being supported by vehicle it has to wait in the car park at 942303.

D. Leave the hamlet of Killilan on the metalled road (W) for 1.5 kilometres, crossing the River Ling on the road bridge.

E. Turn right, up the private road to Nonach Lodge (walkers permitted).

F. Pass the Lodge drive, and go on to the bungalow and barn. Swing right and pass between the two, to gain the pedestrian gate in the fence.

W. It may be possible to reduce the amount of lane-walking by turning left at 969280, walking to the buildings at X and following the path to Canas-luinie at Y. Then follow the lane to the definitive route at Z. (OS indicates that a vehicle could travel to Canas-luinie for a rendezvous.)

NOTE! We have NOT researched the variant WXYZ, so we cannot guarantee its viability.

THE BAGPIPES cont.

a valved tube; it has a reed pipe, or chanter, with finger holes, rather like a recorder, on which the melody notes are played and, usually, three reeded drone pipes, to supply an accompaniment.

Before it reached Scotland the bagpipe was played in England for many centuries, certain counties becoming renowned for the expertise of their pipers. Shakespeare wrote about the drone of the Lincolnshire instrument. Worcestershire, Nottinghamshire and Lancashire pipers have also been documented by artists and writers down the years. The instrument is now nearly extinct in most of England, with the notable exception of Northumberland. In this county, the pipe, unlike its Scottish counterpart, is designed for indoor use and has a gentler tone somewhere between the sound of an oboe and a clarinet. Different from the Scottish version, its air comes from arm-driven bellows.

Over the border from Northumberland is the Lowland Scottish Pipe, also bellows-filled, but otherwise like the pipes in the north and Highlands. The Highland, or Great Pipe, introduced into Scotland early in the fifteenth century, is the one now known worldwide. It exists in three categories: great, half-size and small. If it can be said to have a musical key then it is A major, but this A major comes with a natural G (a little sharpened), and with the C and F tuned between sharp and natural: truly a unique scale, though similar ones are found in the Near Eastern countries. Its range covers nine notes, G to A: one octave plus a note. Until the eighteenth century, there were only two drones. Now there are three, generally two As (low and high) and a D.

The first steps in playing the bagpipe are simple. The drones are thrown over the left shoulder. The bag is held beneath the left arm; the blow-pipe placed to the lips and the chanter held in the fingers of both hands. The piper starts to march, blowing into the pipe. The drones and chanter wail into unharmonious torrents of strident sound. Here, the simplicity ends, as the piper has to entice a melodic line from the chanter. And therein lies the problem. Even though there are only nine notes, the technique of playing the instrument is very difficult to perfect. As the chanter and drones are open pipes they speak continually, allowing legato playing only. This leads players to add grace notes between the melodic ones. Accomplished pipers insert these 'warblers' with great dexterity, often to such an extent that the shape of the melody is lost to untutored ears. It is the unusual scale intervals, the vigorous tone and the profuse embellishments which can sound unmusical to the uninitiated.

Learning to play the pipe is no easy task. As well as mastering the complexity of playing, students have to understand its peculiar ancient musical notation. Known as the Canntaireachd, syllables stand for groups of notes.

An apprenticeship to piping lasts for at least seven years, starting by learning to play the chanter on its own. In Skye, the famous MacCrimmons (1500-1795), for three centuries pipers to the Clan MacLeod, ran a 'college of pipers' in which the students practised in caves. There have been many such colleges over the years.

The repertoire falls into three categories: the Cèol beag 'little music', such as marches, reels and strathspeys; the Cèol meadhonach 'middle music', comprising laments, folksongs, lullabies and slow marches; and the Cèol Mór 'big music', embracing laments, salutes and compositions written for historical occasions. This last category is known, in Anglicised form, as the Pibroch, from the Gaelic *Piobaireachd*.

Both Kings and commoners have become accomplished pipers. Clan chiefs had, and clans still have, their own pipers. The sound of the pipes has been used for many functions, including synchronising the actions of road builders, construction workers and boat launching. Pipes are heard at events like funerals and weddings. Municipal pipers abound and most towns have their pipe bands. But, it is in the armed forces where the Highland Pipe has had the greatest prominence. In 1689 two drummers and a piper were assigned to each and every Scottish infantry regiment, and this association with the pipe has been maintained. Pipes have often played a significant role in raising the spirits of troops going into battle. Some say that their sound instilled foreboding into the hearts of enemy troops; some maintain this was mere conjecture.

Bagpipe music is not to everyone's taste but, like it or loathe it, the pipe has become a national symbol of Scottish culture. It is played with patriotic pride and is here to stay. After a hard day's walking you may be lucky enough, as we once were, to be piped in to dinner. Advancing on your plate of haggis, neaps an' tatties, accompanied, perhaps, by the traditional dram, you may care to reflect on the historical associations evoked by tartaned figures playing the Great Pipe in that never-to-be-forgotten style.

The Master of the Glen

SEVENTH STAGE:
Killilan to Strathcarron
16.5 kilometres, 10.2 miles

To the one of us, who is inherently an untidy person, the spartan tidiness of Killilan is eerie. It has a Marie Celeste atmosphere, enhanced by the large, unoccupied 'hotel or shooting lodge'. Unfortunately, the village is not big enough to support a shop and a pub, but we know from personal experience that the people are as welcoming and friendly as anywhere in Scotland and that is what matters.

Walking up the drive to Nonach Lodge, one feels like an intruder, but walkers are welcome, as we were when we encountered a retired gillie who gave us lots of information. We like to engage in conversation with the local residents, as we find them very chatty and always willing to help.

SEVENTH STAGE

Killilan to Strathcarron

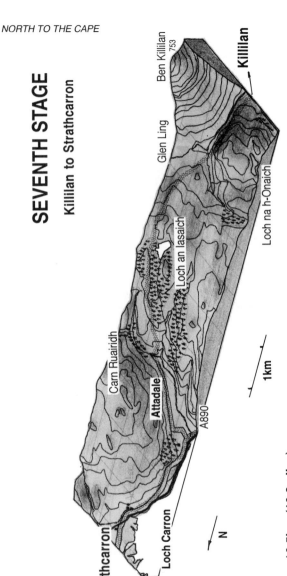

Ben Killilan
753

Glen Ling

Killilan

Loch na h-Onaich

Loch an Iasaich

Carn Ruairidh

Attadale

A890

Strathcarron

Loch Carron

N

1km

16.5km (10.2miles)

Beside the lodge, there is a bungalow beyond which you leave enclosed land to begin the ascent of Glen Ling. Initially the glen is quite narrow, but it soon opens out until the massive western shoulder of Ben Killilan lies on your right. Ahead, lower hills beckon.

After crossing the footbridge over a tributary burn, you begin to climb gently out of Glen Ling. Turn around for a last look down the glen towards Killilan and Loch Long before passing over the summit, beyond which you enter a forest.

West of and close to the route, just as the descent begins, there is a beautiful lochan, Loch an Iasaich, which is well worth a deviation. We found it to be an angler's paradise and a place to sit and dream for a while. We had our lunch there.

Back on the route the first descending kilometre is in the forest, so the scenery is obscured. But lower down, a view over Attadale to Loch Carron presents itself. Attadale House has beautiful gardens, open to visitors from time to time.

Joining the A890, the route follows this road to Strathcarron where there is a shop and an hotel. A few hundred metres beyond the hotel, on the main road, there is B & B accommodation.

The multitude of hillocks, lochans, mini gorges and waterfalls around Attadale and Strathcarron is inviting, so you may want to explore these before moving on.

Additionally, you cannot have missed the railway and station at Strathcarron; this line links Inverness with the Kyle of Lochalsh, and hence the Isle of Skye. Why not have a rest and take a day trip to the Kyle? Had the ferry still been in existence, you could have crossed the Kyle and, at least, set foot on the Isle if not much further.

If you wish to break your journey and return home, the railway at Strathcarron provides the ideal opportunity for you to catch trains to Inverness and onwards. You can, of course, return at your convenience to complete the walk.

Map 7.1

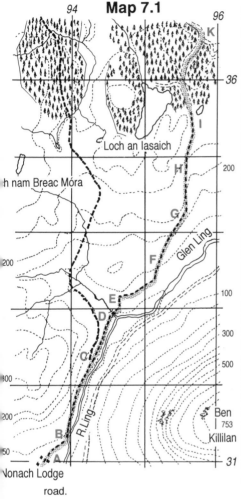

7.1

A. Having passed through the pedestrian gate, bear slightly right into the field. Then turn slightly left to walk parallel to the fence on your left to the field corner, at which you exit the field through a primitive gate.

B. The path is now quite well defined.

C. The path bifurcates at a point which is unclear on the ground. However, it is roughly adjacent to waterfalls on the River Ling. Keep to the lower, right-hand, path near the riverside.

D. Do NOT attempt to ford the incoming burn, but go upstream some 100 metres to the footbridge which is not visible from the River Ling.

E. The path is unclear after the bridge but, if you diverge NW from the River Ling, the path becomes well defined after about 100 metres and keeps to the contour.

FGH. Keep ascending the well-defined path.

I. Enter the forest area through an iron gate near a lochan on your right. The path is very boggy before reaching the forest road. (*)

J. Descend on the forest road.

K. At the junction with the estate road, keep left.

(*) At 955359 a forest road bears left from the route. This leads to beautiful Loch an Iasaich, which is obviously used by anglers and well worth a visit. A good place for lunch!

7.2

AB. Follow the forest/estate road down to, and along, Attadale.

C. Turn left. Do NOT enter the grounds of Attadale House unless you want to visit the gardens.

D. Turn right at the A890.

E. Follow the road to Strathcarron.

Map 7.2

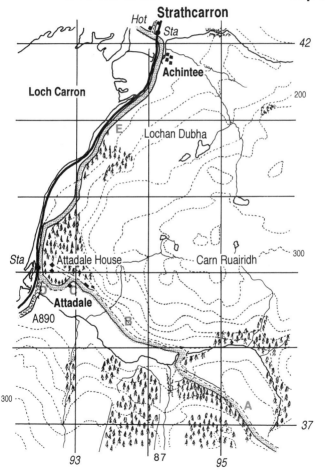

Wood Sculpture

EIGHTH STAGE:
Strathcarron to Achnashellach Station
(SEE VARIANT WARNING)
10.5 kilometres, 6.5 miles

From Strathcarron, you will require provisions for two days if not staying at Achnashellach Lodge.

Our original idea for the route did not include Strathcarron and tried to avoid road walking. It would also have necessitated an extra camp. But, due to broken footbridges, there was no realistic alternative to this march on the A890. As always, a road walk in the West Highlands is no great hardship. There is little traffic and the scenery is majestic. An additional advantage to the definitive route is the accommodation at Strathcarron and the shop. Also it gives you the opportunity to have an easy day, which we always find very welcome. The total ascent is only about 50 metres.

The floor of the strath is an alluvial flat which carries some cultivation, including forestry. However its sides are very steep, especially the south-

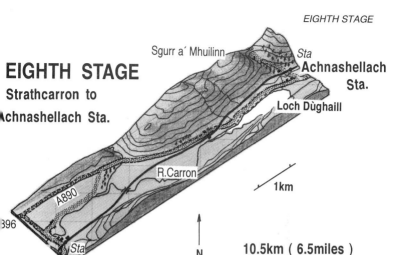

EIGHTH STAGE

**Strathcarron to
Achnashellach Sta.**

Sgurr a´ Mhuilinn

Sta
**Achnashellach
Sta.**

Loch Dùghaill

R.Carron

A890

1km

396

Sta

rathcarron

N

10.5km (6.5miles)

eastern side rising up to Corn Mór and then up to Eagan. The north-western flank rises less steeply at first, but it's very steep up to Fuor Tholl beyond which are the Torridans. The River Carron, meaning 'winding stream', meanders through the 1.5 kilometre-wide strath, giving its name to glen, strath and sea loch. It is joined at Achnashellach by the River Lair which drains the Coulin (deer) forest to the north-west and flows into Loch Dùghaill fed by the River Strath.

There is accommodation at Achnashellach Lodge, but no shop. This community takes its name from the railway station.

You must have noticed that you could use the train (time tables permitting) to get from Strathcarron to Achnashellach Lodge and thus avoid the road walk. If you do use the train, you are definitely cheating.

Map 8.1

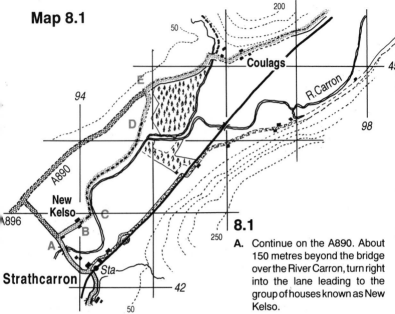

8.1

A. Continue on the A890. About 150 metres beyond the bridge over the River Carron, turn right into the lane leading to the group of houses known as New Kelso.

B. After the last house, pass through the gate into the field and continue ahead to the River Carron.

C. At the river, turn left and follow the defined path beside the river.

D. Pass through the gate into the forest area and join the track (forest road).

E. Turn right at the A890.

8.2

A. Continue on the A890 to the track leading to Achnashellach Station.

B. Turn sharp left up the track to the station. Cross the railway (through the gates), and turn right to ascend on the track (forest road).

C. After some 100 metres, or so, turn sharp left at the junction with other forest roads.

D. After 300 metres, or so, branch left onto a path. (At the time of research, this path was closed due to forest operations. This necessitated a further, well signed, 150 metres on the forest road before transfer to the path.)

E. Ascend steeply on the well-defined path.

> **VARIANT WARNING**
> **Glen Carron/Strathcarron**
> OS Landranger 25. Glen Carron

We examined the feasibility of a route from the forest above Attadale (957366) along the estate road to Bendronaig Lodge (013389). Then on the path northwards, leaving it to pass the west side of Loch an Laoigh (017415) to join another path at 020429 which ascends and crosses over Eagan. A steep descent follows into Glen Carron to reach the River Carron opposite Achnashellach Station.

HOWEVER, WE DISCOVERED THAT THE FOOTBRIDGE SHOWN ON OS HAD FALLEN DOWN, NECESSITATING THE FORDING OF A DANGEROUS, DEEP, SWIFT FLOWING, WIDE RIVER.

Therefore, we decided to abandon this magnificent route. OS shows a bridge at 048494, accessible by a 4 kilometre plod on a forest road followed by a march of the same distance on the A890 back to Achnashellach. Try it if you want!

Map 8.2

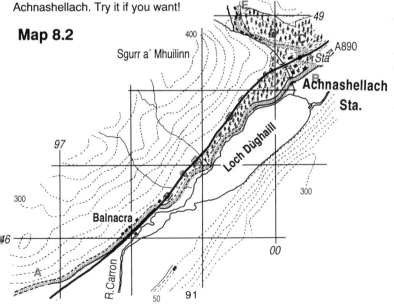

BOTHIES AND THE MBA

Britain's bothies need cherishing. The current guardians of a large number of them are the members of the Mountain Bothies Association (MBA). The stated objective of the MBA is: 'To maintain simple unlocked shelters in remote country for the use and benefit of all those who love wild and lonely places'. Bothy is an eighteenth century Scottish word defined as 'a small hut or cottage for housing labourers'. Its origin is obscure, but it may be related to 'booth'.

In the early nineteenth century, as one of the consequences of Bonnie Prince Charlie's defeat at Culloden in 1746, the Highland Clearances took place. Many simple thatched cottages were put to the torch and, without roofs, the stonework quickly deteriorated. Eventually the walls fell down. Some families remained in the remote glens, employed as gillies, stalkers and servants and housed in new, much improved, dwellings. The new housing, superior to the old thatched cottages, had mortared walls, wooden floors, slate roofs and glass in the windows. It did not have such luxuries as running water or sanitation.

Nearly two hundred years later, World War II was to change matters yet again. As the war progressed, many young Britons were conscripted to serve in the armed forces. They came home with fresh views of the world. Dissatisfied with the solitude and penury of their upbringing, the youth of the glens moved south to seek work. In a matter of five years, a whole generation had migrated.

The war also saw the invention of the Willys Jeep, a small sturdy motor vehicle with emergency four-wheel drive. After the war came its successor the Land Rover, which revolutionised estate practices. Its potential was soon exploited by landowners, whose workers no longer had to live in remote places. Using these vehicles, they could transport themselves and the materials of their trade to and from the worksite with little difficulty.

Another aftermath of the war was soaring economic growth in Europe in general and in Britain in particular. Working hours decreased and wages escalated. Workers now had the time and could afford to engage in outdoor pursuits, no longer the preserve of the rich.

So, there was a situation where vacant properties were available for hill walkers and there were hill walkers who wanted to use them. In the '60s, interest in outdoor pursuits increased. Walkers packed the Pennine Way and Munro bagging burgeoned. While these numbers rose, the bothies were falling into ruin. With a few exceptions, only ad hoc maintenance had been carried out. Something had to be done.

Bernard Heath, a Huddersfield man like ourselves, had spent many years cycling and walking in Scotland. In 1965, prompted by suggestions from others, Heath grasped the initiative and organised the inaugural meeting of the MBA in Dalmellington Village, Galloway: the previous summer had seen the restoration of Tunskeen, a cottage in the Galloway hills. During the following year, work started in earnest to restore bothies. The MBA has grown a lot since those early days. It currently has about 2,400 members scattered throughout Britain, plus a few from abroad. Area Committees manage bothies grouped together geographically. In addition to the Management Committees, there are subcommittees dealing with such important matters as Health and Safety. The MBA now looks after 103 bothies. Currently there are seventy-one in the Highlands and Islands; eleven in Southern Scotland; fourteen in Northern England and the Borders and seven in Wales. The Association is strictly a maintenance organisation, not a user's club, and it is always keen to see new volunteers on its work parties. Not all bothies are maintained by the MBA; some are privately cared for. It should be noted that the word 'bothy' on a map does not differentiate between a well-maintained bothy and one that is in ruins.

The MBA is a charity, funded through members' subscriptions, donations and bequests. Occasionally, a grant will be obtained from another organisation or trust to help fund a particular project. It does not own any bothies. Each bothy remains the property of and is maintained with the permission of the landowner. Anyone may use the bothies, although they cannot be booked in advance. However, the Association has a policy of discouraging group use. Large groups (over six) should obtain the owner's permission before lodging in a bothy, except in case of emergency. And it should be remembered that some bothies are only big enough to accommodate two or three visitors comfortably. Needless to say, individuals and groups planning to use a bothy, and especially a popular or small one, should carry a tent and be prepared to use it.

Bothies are usually unlocked, but some owners may lock them during the stalking season. Bothies may be closed if the owner decides that the level of use results in vandalism, sanitation problems or non-observation of, for example, stalking restrictions.

The MBA publishes a Newsletter four times a year and, once a year, an updated list of bothies. The local contact and details of any restrictions are included. Grid references of bothies are not published. Until a few years ago, the Association gave all new members a list, with grid references. This was stopped when increased use brought in its wake bouts of vandalism and sanitation problems. Map publishers have been asked to delete references to bothies in order to limit visitors to manageable proportions. As members and supporters of the Outdoor Writers' Guild (OWG), and in accordance with the agreement between the MBA and the OWG, we have, with one exception, refrained from identifying bothies on our Stage and Navigation Maps. The exception is where a bothy is strategically placed (by coincidence), and we feel that not to mention it would be a disservice to our readers. Safety considerations are also relevant. This does NOT mean that other bothies do not exist. Any serious, sympathetic walker can receive information about the location of bothies by contacting the MBA. We have included a contact address and telephone number in the Appendix C.

Like all charities, the MBA relies on goodwill for funding as well as help with the physical work of maintenance. Bothies can only continue to exist if those who use them help to look after them. We entreat our readers to abide by the Bothy Code:

BOTHY CODE

Respect Other Users
- Please leave the bothy clean, tidy and with dry kindling for the next visitors.

Respect The Bothy
- Guard against fire risk and don't cause vandalism or graffiti.
- Please take out **all** rubbish which you don't burn. Avoid burying rubbish: this pollutes the environment. Please don't leave perishable food: this encourages mice and rats.

Respect The Surroundings
- Human waste must be buried carefully out of sight - please use the spade provided. For health reasons, never use the vicinity of the

bothy as a toilet and keep well away from the water supply.
• Conserve fuel. Never cut live wood.

Please Note:

Bothies are available for short stays only, normally of only a few days. Permission should be obtained for long stays.

Unless the safety of the group requires the use of shelter in bad weather, bothies are not available for large groups of six or more because of overcrowding and the lack of facilities such as toilets. For the same reasons, groups are asked not to camp outside bothies. Groups wishing to use a bothy should seek permission from the estate.

Finally, please ensure the fire is out and the door properly closed when you leave.

Bothies are used at your own risk

As professional walkers, we have spent a lifetime visiting wild and lonely places. Whilst we understand the dilemma the MBA is in, we feel that a knowledge of the precise whereabouts of bothies would be a decided advantage. In cases of emergency which, by definition, cannot be predetermined, a bothy could be a lifesaver ONLY if one knows where it is. Bothies near to other habitations are, perhaps, less of an asset. However it is up to us, the users. If we ALL respect and abide by the Bothy Code, then there will be fewer problems. May the MBA continue to concentrate on what it does best: 'Maintaining simple unlocked shelters in remote country for the use and benefit of those who love wild and lonely places'.

Bienn Eighe

NINTH STAGE:
Achnashellach Station to Kinlochewe (See Variant 9)
17.0 kilometres, 10.5 miles

We know next to nothing about geology, so our perception of the landscape is that of an observant walker and amateur geographer. Consequently, we have divided the country through which our route passes into three areas: the southern area running from Loch Eil to Glen Carron, which we call Knoydart; the mid area running from Glen Carron to Loch Broom, which we call The Torridons; and the northern area, which we call Assynt. Nevertheless, we do recognise the section between Glen Shiel and Glen Carron as a transition one, as we do that between Dundonell and Glen Oykel.

Our perception is based on our observation of the shape of the mountains and of their texture, even though we realise this is too

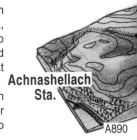

96

simplistic for the professionals. Doubtless one could engage in long hours of academic discussion of the merits of our classification, but we feel it serves our purpose adequately.

Thus, this ninth stage is the first in the Torridon region and its entry is awesome. The ascent out of Glen Carron presents a steady climb along a well-defined, well-maintained, but very rough path, with fine backward views. The nearby river descends the steep gorge in bouncing waterfalls, but you will have to leave the path to see them.

At the bealach, the south face of Beinn Liath Mhór dominates your north-west view, while south-west lies the cone of Fuar Tholl. Three paths leave the bealach; ours is north-north-east, ascending to Coulin. The path leaving west-south-west gives access to Fuar Tholl and that going west-north-west follows the glen under Beinn Liath Mhór. This is one of those places where we sometimes wish we were not doing a long distance walk and could go off route and explore.

Back to business: our descent is super, with lovely views ahead. Lower down there are scatterings of Scots Pines which might be remnants of the ancient Caledonian forest once covering Scotland. Lower still, the glen opens out and the walking is on a well-made track capable of carrying four-wheel drive vehicles.

The cottages at Coulin appear to have been renovated recently, so

NINTH STAGE
Achnashellach Sta. to Kinlochewe

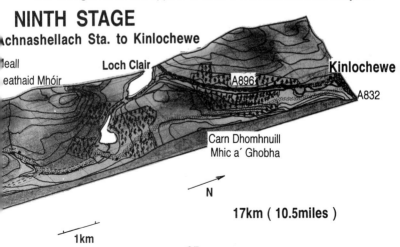

17km (10.5miles)

1km

are in good condition. Beyond Torran-cuilinn, the climb is gentle but goes through forestry land where the path is very wet and not well defined. In contrast to the climb from Achnashellach Station, this one is rather dull. Beyond the forest, the path becomes well defined and open, with elegant views. As you start the descent, the white quartzite on the summit of Beinn Eighe (rhymes with 'ache' and means 'the file') sparkles like snow to the west-north-west. The formal route descends through a forest, but the going is difficult (See Map Notes 9.2). The last two kilometres into Kinlochewe are straightforward, running beside the river (A' Ghainbhe), and make a very pleasant end to a fine day's walk.

Kinlochewe means 'the head of Loch Ewe', but it is at the head of Loch Maree. Hundreds of years ago Loch Maree, dominated by the powerful presence of Slioch (meaning 'a spear'), was known as Loch Ewe. The name was changed to distinguish it from the sea loch into which it flows. The new name was taken from St Maelrubha who was buried on Isle Maree, one of the loch's wooded islands, in the seventh century. The Isle was a place of pilgrimage for many centuries. Queen Victoria visited in 1877 and made her wish at the wishing tree. There are still remains of the Saint's monastery, the wishing well (now filled in) and the tree.

There is an hotel at Kinlochewe, as well as a campsite and B & Bs. There are also shops for provisions. You could stay a week and more to explore the surrounding mountains and the Beinn Eighe National Nature Reserve, via the Visitor Centre. We did once.

9.1

A.   Ascend on the well-defined path.

B.   Keep right at each branch in the path.

C.   Descend on the well-defined path.

D.   Lunch at the shelter?

E.   Keep ahead and left. Do NOT cross the bridge.

F.   Turn right just before the smart estate cottages.

G.   Cross the River Coulin on the bridge and continue towards the cottage.

H.   Turn left before the cottage gate. No path.

I.   Cross the small burn where you can and make for the forest fence. Rough going. Do NOT follow the defined track into the forest.

J.   Keep parallel to the fence, proceeding NW. Pass through the gate. At first no path is visible and the going is very rough through long grass and across ruts. Aim generally N, making for another fence on your left.

K.   Ascend, keeping the fence on your left. Boggy path, defined in places.

Map 9.1

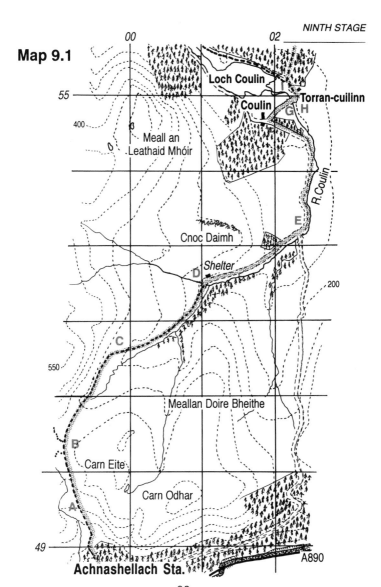

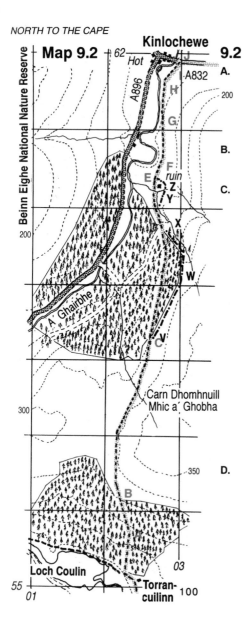

Map 9.2

9.2

A. Continue to ascend, crossing two forest roads. Path defined in places and very wet. The direction is clear; simply keep to the ride.

B. Leave the forest at the gate and follow the defined path across the moor.

C. Formally the path enters the forest, but at the time of research (spring 1997), blown trees made progress very difficult if not impossible. (It took us about one hour to fight our way through this one-and-a-half kilometres of forest.) We found out later that the landowner had erected notices warning walkers of the problem and advising them not to enter the forest, but to proceed outside along the eastern fence, and around VWX, adding not more then 100 metres or so to the route. We found no notices, but advise walking round if you have any doubt about the formal route (*).

D. On reaching the gate in the forest fence, proceed more or less N (outside the forest), keeping the burn on your right and the forest fence on your left. OS shows a burn crossing place lower down, but we found this difficult so we suggest crossing as soon as you can. However, this will require the crossing of a second burn (YZ).

E. Get to the ruins and then proceed N. Path undefined.

F. Pass through the gate, after which the path is defined.

G. Descend to the riverside. Pass through the gate, and continue on the defined path to the next gate.

H. Turn NNE to cross the field to the far gate.

I. The track to the road is boggy, but the way is obvious.

J. At the road, turn left into the village of Kinlochewe or right to continue.

(*) It seems that a group of pedants caused the notices to be removed. We consider this to be an act of utmost irresponsibility, as inexperienced walkers could become disorientated and lost in the forest with the possibility of fatality.

Variant 9: **Achnashellach Station to Coulin**
8 kilometres, 5 miles
OS Landranger 25. Glen Carron

This route is shorter than the definitive one, on a well-defined track all the way. It does not reach the same height and is thus faster. It is suitable for bad weather conditions, but is far less interesting.

Leave the station on the definitive route, but instead of taking the left turn, keep ahead to ascend the forest road. Make sure you ascend. Do NOT take the lower road parallel with the railway.

Simply follow the forest road/track over the Coulin Pass (023503), descend and join the definitive route across the bridge at - 023531 Then turn right and on to Coulin.

MILITARY ROADS

> If you had seen these roads before they were made
> You would hold up your hands and bless General Wade

(anon)

Probably the most common structures built by the Romans were roads. Originally built for military purposes, the roads had a significant effect on the civil population and the Roman trunk road system at the height of the Empire covered some 90,000 kilometres. Not straight throughout their length, as is popularly supposed, Roman roads consisted of a series of straight sections which deviated to avoid obstructions. The roads, many still in use today, were usually constructed in three or four layers to ensure adequate drainage and stability. The top layer was paved and also cambered, to allow surface water to drain into the ditches at each side.

During their stay in Britain, AD 43 to AD 407, the Romans built many roads, making London the focus of the communication system. This was the earliest skilled attempt at nationwide road making in this country, and many of our modern roads follow the old Roman lines. Their most important roads were: Watling Street, from Dover to London, then to Chester and Holyhead; Ermine Street, from London to York; Foss Way, from Dorchester to Lincoln, and Akeman Street, from London to Cirencester. As the Romans never conquered the Highlands of Scotland, no roads were built by them in this area.

After the Roman era, road making in Britain fell into decay until the onset of the Industrial Revolution. In the mid-eighteenth century, fresh attempts were made to provide good highways. The Turnpike Acts provided for the reconstruction of many kilometres of road, the cost being met by tolls.

Scotland had its own special problems around this time: the Fifteen and the Forty-five Jacobite Rebellions. In July 1724, Major-General George Wade (1673 - 1748), English soldier and Member of Parliament for Bath, was dispatched to Scotland. His mission was "to narrowly inspect the present situation of the Highlanders ... to make strict enquiry into the law for disarming the Highlanders ... to suggest to His Majesty such other remedies as may conduce to the good settlement of that part of the Kingdom".

Wade reported that the situation was in a shambles. The companies of the Highland army were defrauding the Government, the barracks were undermanned and "The Highlands are still more impracticable from the want of roads and bridges". Wade was appointed Commander-in-Chief, North Britain, on Christmas Eve 1724. In the spring of 1725, he pressed for a new 'Disarming Act', aimed at effectively drawing the teeth of the Highlanders following the Fifteen; six more companies, to join the regular troops; two regiments to man the forts and barracks; five companies to garrison Edinburgh and Leith; money for repairing the garrisons at Edinburgh and Fort William and for building new forts at Killichuimen and Inverness. Most significantly, he asked for £10,000 for each of two years for camp provisions, to pay the troops and to mend the roads between the garrisons and the barracks and "for the better Communication of His Majesty's Troops". Little did Wade realise the consequences of this last request.

The Government, impressed by Wade's proposals, passed a new Disarming Act and sent him back to Scotland in June 1725, to implement the Act and to repair the roads. Wade set about removing all weapons from the wily clans, but was not very successful. Nevertheless, he built a boat, the Highland Galley, to carry troops about Loch Ness. He repaired the forts and castles. He repaired the barracks but, above all, he will be remembered for his success at road building. Some roads were realigned to make gradients or bends less severe. New bridges were built, as were many kilometres of new road. Wade's major roads were: Fort William to Inverness (98 kilometres); Dunkeld to Inverness (164 kilometres); Crieff to Dalnacardoch (69 kilometres). He built a total of 383 kilometres as well as many bridges.

In 1739, the Government decided that matters in Scotland were "well under control". Wade was recalled, promoted to full General, made a Privy Councillor in 1744 and promoted Field-Marshall the following year. He spent the rest of his years as Commander-in-Chief in the Low Counties and in England. He died at the age of 75, left a fortune of more than £100,000 and is buried in Westminster Abbey. That was the end of Marshall Wade, but it was not the end of military roads.

It is often supposed that Wade made all the military roads. This was not so. He was succeeded in Scotland by Lieutenant-General Clayton, who inherited Wade's Inspector of Roads, Major William Caulfeild. They carried on the good work. Notwithstanding the defeat of Bonnie Prince Charlie and his Jacobite followers at Culloden in 1746, the military presence in Scotland was increased. Jacobite estates were taken over, and their rents and profits applied "for the better civilising and improving the Highlands of Scotland and preventing disorders there". A more severe Disarming Act was passed. Tartan, the kilt and bagpipes were forbidden. Castles, forts, garrisons and barracks were fully manned so that the repressive measures could be ruthlessly enforced. The authority of the Clan Chiefs and big landowners was destroyed as they were gradually transformed into 'mere' landlords. The demilitarisation of Highland life broke ties which had been established over generations, and the clansmen became tenants and cottars. But the road building went on.

Following Wade's departure, Caulfeild planned and built 1,290 kilometres of road, and more, in the Highlands. His greatest achievements were roads from Bridge of Sark to Fort Patrick (169 kilometres), Couper Angus to Fort George (161 kilometres), Stirling to Fort William (150 kilometres), Stonehaven to Fochabars by Aberdeen (135 kilometres) and Fettercairn to Fochabars (106 kilometres). Caulfeild died in 1767. A further 160 kilometres were built before the military communication system in Scotland was considered satisfactory.

Both Wade and Caulfeild used the Roman system of construction, utilising readily-available raw materials. After digging the foundations, big stones were levered and winched into a 4.88 metre-wide trench. Smaller stones were packed on top, followed by a layer of gravel at least 0.6 metre deep. The whole lot was tamped down using shovels, hammers and human feet. As the surface was not paved, replenishment and repacking of the gravel was a yearly event, at the least. Despite the provision of drains on each side of the road, some sections were to be washed away by the inevitable waterfalls rushing down the mountainsides. Replacement of these top surfaces was even more frequent.

In Roman times, the roads were used by military and populace alike. However, some of the more obdurate Highlanders initially refused to use the military roads, preferring to exercise their independence along their established routes. Where these coincided with a new road, they would walk alongside the road fording the rivers and ignoring the bridges.

In 1801, Thomas Telford (1757 - 1834) the famous Scottish Civil Engineer, was commissioned by the Government to report on and follow up with public works required for Scotland. He constructed the Caledonian

Canal and 1,600 kilometres of road with 1,200 bridges in Scotland. He is said to have been very impressed by the original works of Wade and Caulfeild.

During your journey up the Western Highlands, you will walk on military roads at three points. Passing through Fort William is the first of Wade's products, the Great Glen road; constructed between 1725 and 1727, this road runs from Fort William to Inverness, a distance of 98 kilometres. At Shiel Bridge, you will walk on the A87, originally a Caulfeild road built between 1755 and 1763 and joining Fort Augustus with Bernera, a distance of 69 kilometres.

There were barracks at Bernera guarding the shortest crossing to Skye across the Kyle Rhea. The origins of the road from Contin via Kinlochewe (through which you will pass) to Poolewe are, unfortunately, somewhat obscure. There is no firm evidence that there was a road for the whole 84 kilometres. However, the balance of opinion is that one was built by Caulfeild between 1761 and 1763.

You will not find Caulfeild's name in many biographical dictionaries. But, he should always be remembered for his skill, knowledge and foresight in establishing the basis of the Highland road system we know today.

Lochan Fada

TENTH STAGE:
Kinlochewe to Loch an Nid (See Variant 10)
17.1 kilometres, 10.6 miles

From Kinlochewe you will require provisions for three days if you are visiting Ullapool and eleven days if not; although it may be possible to arrange meals at the hotels at Oykel Bridge (end of Stage Fourteen), Inchnadamph (end of Stage Sixteen) and Kylesku (end of Stage Seventeen).

This may be the most difficult stage in the whole route. Despite the snow-capped mountains and magnificent April weather with which we were privileged, it took us seven hours to walk the 17.1 kilometres (10.6 miles) involved.

The walk from Kinlochewe to the footbridge over the Abhainn an Fhasaigh begins through farmland, then joins the banks of the Kinlochewe River and, later, the side of Loch Maree. Beinn Eighe dominates, south-west.

TENTH STAGE

Kinlochewe to Loch an Nid

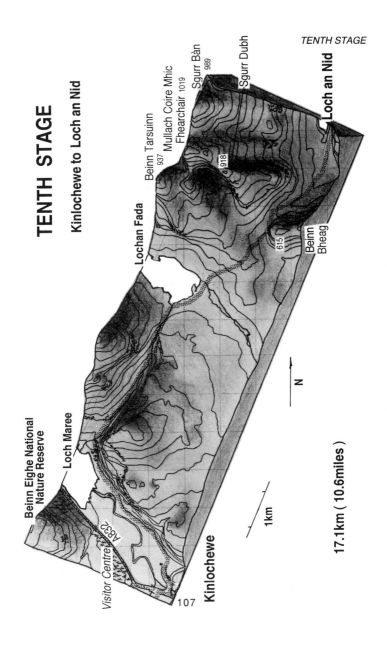

107

Beinn Eighe National
Nature Reserve

Loch Maree

A832

Visitor Centre

Kinlochewe

Lochan Fada

Beinn Tarsuinn
937

Mullach Coire Mhic
Fhearchair 1019

Sgurr Bàn
989

Sgurr Dubh

918

615

Beinn
Bheag

Loch an Nid

N

1km

17.1km (10.6miles)

The ascent of Gleann Bianasdail is very rough despite the defined path most of the way. The first kilometre, additionally, is very wet on peat. Take great care when crossing the river as it flows out of Lochan Fada. This can be the most difficult crossing of the whole trek; it can also be rather dangerous after a period of heavy rain because of the high flow rate and rocky bed.

As you walk along the shore of Lochan Fada turn to look along its length. Half left rises Slioch to 980 metres and in the distance, on each side of this glacial valley, rise the mountains of Letterewe Forest. These hills were once heavily forested, but the only remnants are to be found on the shore of Loch Maree. As early as 1605, oaks were being harvested to provide charcoal for iron ore smelters. By the mid-nineteenth century, most of the forest had been ravaged to supply the hungry furnaces which were supplied with ore from over 1,500 veins working in this area.

When you leave Lochan Fada the climb

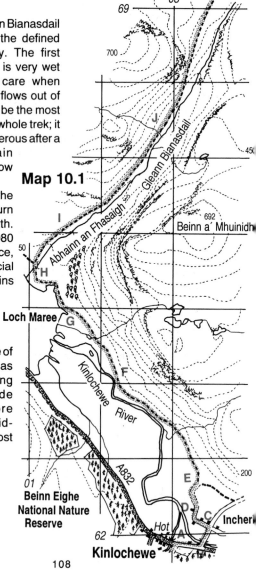

Map 10.1

108

is not steep, but there is no formal path and the going is harsh and wet in places. On reaching Loch Meallan an Fhùdair, look north to see both the massif of Mullach Coire Mhic Fhearchair (1019 metres) and Sgurr Dubh (918 metres). Watch your navigation when leaving the loch to get to Bealach na Croise, otherwise you may descend into the wrong glen. The bealach will feel very closed in and isolated.

Afterwards, the descent continues to be very arduous in a narrow gorge. But you will be rewarded by a smooth, close-cropped grazing ahead of Loch an Nid which is ideal for your camp. Having set up, look westwards at the dramatic, enormous slabs; very dangerous in icy conditions.

10.1

A. Leave Kinlochewe E on the A832.

B. Turn left towards Incheril and cross the Kinlochewe River.

C. Turn left where the lanes cross. Follow the lane, which degenerates to a track.

D. Pass through the farmyard and keep left. The right fork leads to the cemetery.

E. Pass through the gate and join the path.

F. Follow the well-defined path.

G. Keep to the lower path near to Loch Maree. An (unofficial?) path climbs up through trees as if to make a short cut. We do NOT recommend it!

H. Ascend to and cross the footbridge, then keep right. A rough boggy climb.

I. Soft ground. Path not well defined.

J. The path in the gorge is rough but defined.

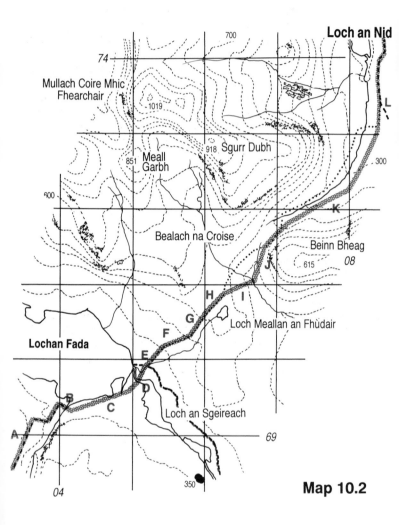

Map 10.2

10.2

A. At the highest point, the path becomes undefined. Keep ahead (ENE) towards Lochan Fada before turning E to descend. The path becomes defined.

B. Cross the river where you can, near to where it leaves the lochan. It is of the order of 0.5 metre deep in places, so you may get your feet and legs wet unless you have exceptional protective clothing. A stout stick, to form a third support point, could be very handy at this crossing.

C. Keep to the shore of the lochan. There is a fairly well-defined path.

D. A much easier crossing. Then follow the path easterly.

E. About 100 metres from the lochan and just before a burn, turn left (ENE) to leave the path.

F. Ascend, keeping the burn on your right. No path.

G. OS shows the burn clearly leaving Loch Meallan an Fhùdair. However, as you ascend, the multiplicity of watercourses makes it difficult to identify the main one on the ground. Use your compass to ascend NE.

H. It is CRUCIAL that you find this small loch, in order to get a navigational fix. Failure to do so may mean that you descend into the wrong glen. Keep to the left of the loch.

I. Choose your own route (ENE) and descend. No identifiable best route. Rough everywhere.

J. Ascend gently to the bealach with its cairn.

K. Descend NE. No path. Despite there being a path of sorts on the NW side of the burn, we recommend keeping to the SE side thus avoiding a difficult river crossing lower down.

L. Join the well-defined path which comes in from the SE. There are good camping places hereabouts.

Variant 10: **Kinlochewe to Lochan Fada**
10.4 kilometres, 6.5 miles
OS Landranger 19. Gairloch and Ullapool Area

This is about the same distance as the definitive route. It is on a track for about two-thirds of the way, the remainder being on a defined gentle path, probably wet in places. Useful as a bad weather route, it also avoids the possibly difficult river crossing at Lochan Fada.

Leave Kinlochewe on the definitive route, but at -

034621	keep ahead on the metalled lane to its end at -
039624	Then join the track, following it to the Heights of Kinlochewe at -
072641	Keep LEFT to ascend NNE, crossing the river bridge at -
074653	Continue on the track. At its end at -
070668	keep ahead on the path, parallel with the river. At -
052699	turn right to join the definitive route and ascend.

PRINCE CHARLES EDWARD LOUIS PHILIP CASIMIR STUART

Prince Charles Edward Louis Philip Casimir Stuart was known variously as 'The Young Pretender', 'The Young Chevalier', and, of course, 'Bonnie Prince Charlie'. He led a hectic, dangerous, exciting, some say glamorous life, ending in desolation. The monument to The Forty-five at Glenfinnan is historically appropriate, and is thought by many to commemorate the Bonnie Prince. However, the stone figure atop the baroque style, grey, round tower is not that of the Prince. It is that of a bearded Highlander, serving as a potent reminder of the intense loyalty shown by the clansmen to the Stuarts.

Bonnie Prince Charlie's name may well call to mind that time in Scottish history when the 25 year-old Prince tried to re-establish the power of the House of Stuart. The family of Stewart had ruled Scotland for 232 years until James VI of Scotland united the two countries when he became James I of England. From this time, the French name, Stuart, was used in connection with the monarchy. The Highland areas of Arisaig and Morar were well known to Charles and his followers; areas now seen in a romantic light, but perhaps seen rather differently during that desperate struggle in the mid-eighteenth century.

James II (1633 - 1701), son of James I, became King of Great Britain and Ireland when he ascended the throne on the death of his brother, Charles II, in 1685. It soon became apparent that James' policies were at variance with those of Parliament. He offended the government in many ways, but two of his deeds actually led to his downfall.

The Test Act, passed by Parliament in 1673, decreed that all those who held public office must receive the Church of England Sacrament and renounce Transubstantiation, thus excluding Nonconformists and

Roman Catholics. James refused to acknowledge this Act, and adopted a pro-Catholic policy.

To further his aspirations, he proclaimed his Declaration of Indulgence in 1687 which, although it freed Dissenters, Protestants and Catholics from discrimination under the law, was rejected by the Catholics as being 'only a trick'. Most churches refused to acknowledge his Declaration, so James took seven prominent bishops to court (Primate Sancroft, Bishops Ken, Lake, Lloyd, Turner, Trelawney and White). This simply added to James' unpopularity. The Bishops were acquitted.

The conflict between Crown and Parliament escalated, leading to the Glorious Revolution in 1688, when seven leading noblemen, so incensed by James' behaviour, invited William and Mary, Prince and Princess of Orange, to come and release the country from its unpopular ruler. Revolts broke out as William landed, but there was little or no bloodshed, and James, taking the line of least resistance, fled. He was captured on board his ship and brought back to London, but proved to be a bit of an embarrassment and was allowed to 'escape'. This time he got to France, where, with Irish and French assistance, he tried to regain his throne. In 1690 William soundly defeated James at the Battle of the Boyne; an event marked annually by the Protestants of Ulster. James returned to France and devoted his life to matters religious. He died at St Germain in 1701.

Back in Britain, William and Mary were crowned joint King and Queen in 1689, and Parliament instituted safeguards to ensure that none of James II's iniquitous philosophies survived. The Lords and the Commons passed a Bill of Rights, which is of exceptional importance in the constitutional history of England but of little relevance to ordinary people. After reciting the misdeeds of James and acknowledging his 'abdication', it declares that:

1. The suspension of laws by regal authority without the consent of Parliament is illegal
2. The power of dispensing with laws by regal authority without the consent of Parliament is illegal
3. The levying of money for the use of the Crown without permission of Parliament is illegal
4. It is the right of a subject to petition the King and all prosecutions for such are illegal
5. That raising and or keeping an army within the kingdom in time of

peace without Parliament's consent is illegal
6. Protestants may have arms for their defence allowed by law
7. Elections of Members of Parliament will be free
8. The freedom of speech and debate in Parliament ought not to be impeached or questioned in any court
9. Excessive bail ought not to be required nor excessive fines imposed nor cruel or unusual punishments inflicted
10. For redress of all grievances and for amending, strengthening and preserving of laws Parliament ought to be held frequently.

The act did not create new law, but was merely a re-statement of the old. This 1689 Bill is still held in the House of Lords Record Office and, at the time of writing, the parchment rolls are undergoing restoration, along with 18,000 others dating back to 1497 during the reign of Henry VII.

James Stuart (1688 - 1766), the only son of James II and Mary of Modena, was taken to France at the time of the Glorious Revolution. On the death of his father, James, known as The Old Pretender, was declared 'King of England' at St Germain by his Jacobite supporters. 'Jacobite' is derived from 'Jacobus', the Latin version of James. Not all Highlanders were Jacobites and not all Jacobites were Highlanders, or even Scots. The Jacobites raised a rebellion in 1715, which became known as The Fifteen. The chief events were the Battles of Sherriffmuir in Scotland, where the Scottish Jacobites were easily beaten, and of Preston, where the English Jacobites suffered a similar fate. James Stuart travelled to Scotland, where he was joined by the Earl of Mar. However, The Fifteen was all but over, so he quickly returned to France. He married Maria Sobieski in 1719 and she became the mother of Prince Charles Edward Stuart, the Young Pretender or Bonnie Prince Charlie as he became known. The name 'Charlie' is not an affectionate diminutive but is the English form of the Gaelic *Tearlaich*, or Charles. Born in 1720, he spent his formative years in Rome.

At the age of 23 his attempt to invade England was unsuccessful. But two years later, on 23 July 1745, Charles, together with 'Seven Men from Moidart', disembarked from the armed brig Du Teillay, at anchor in Loch nan Uamh on the Arisaig coast. MacDonald of Clanranald, whose territory was Morar and Moidart, and Cameron of Lochiel tried to talk Charles into returning to France. Being unsuccessful, they set about raising the clans. Making his way through Moidart by way of Glen Shiel and Glen Aladale, Charles moved to Glenfinnan only to find no supporters awaiting him on that wet Monday morning of 19 August. Charles lost all hope. But later in the day, he was joined by MacDonald and Cameron with a total of 850 men. The Highland Bishop blessed the crimson and white Stuart banner, raised by the Duke of Atholl. The gathering increased in number by the hour. By the end of the day, 5,000 men were assembled, ready, keen and eager to do battle. Charles' despair changed to elation. The Forty-five was about to begin.

Marching south, they took Edinburgh on 17 September, although the castle remained impregnable. On 21 September, 2,000 Jacobites routed the King's forces led by Sir John Cope at Prestonpans; they attacked before Cope's troops were awake. Only one shot was fired, but Cope's entire force was put to the sword or captured. About 140 Highlanders were killed or wounded. Following this triumph, Charles left for London on 1 November but, on reaching Derby on 6 December, the Jacobites were forced to retreat. The Young Pretender's hopes were raised at Falkirk, where he defeated the British led by General Hawley on 16 January 1746. This success was not to be repeated.

The Battle of Culloden, fought at one o'clock on 16 April 1746, the last battle ever to be fought in Britain, brought about the downfall of the Young Pretender. In thirty minutes, the Duke of Cumberland, 'Butcher Cumberland', crushed the Jacobites. They fled Culloden Moor and went into hiding.

Charles spent the next five months desperately trying to avoid capture. With half-a-dozen men, he rode to the castle of MacDonnell of Glengarry on Loch Oich. After a few hours' rest he rode on, with three men, by Loch Arkaig to the house of Cameron of Glen Pean, stopped the night and went on by foot to Loch Morar. In the hope of meeting up with a French ship, he was rowed to Benbecula in the Outer Hebrides. The army and navy, informed of his whereabouts, moved in for the kill. Lady Margaret MacDonald organised his escape, but it was Flora MacDonald who put the plans into action.

Flora MacDonald (1722 - 1790), a long time supporter of Charles, disguised him as her maidservant, Betty Burke, and smuggled him to Portree on Skye. For this act, she was later incarcerated in the Tower of London, where she was much fêted for her heroism, and soon released in 1747. She later emigrated with her husband to America, but died in her native Scotland.

With a price of £30,000 on his head, an enormous sum in those days, Charles was a valuable commodity. Many Highlanders, and others, were tortured to disclose his whereabouts. They held firm, and the romantic stories of Charles' wanderings have survived the ages. He stayed briefly at Morar, with troops swarming everywhere; he spent desperate times hiding in caves and, indeed, one of the caves in Loch nan Uamh, Loch of the Caves, is marked on some maps as 'Prince Charles' Cave'. However, this is unverified and may only be legendary. Charles made a break for the mountains, where he played cat and mouse with the redcoats. Word reached him in September that two French ships were at anchor in Loch nan Uamh. On 19 September 1746 the Prince, with a large company of men, boarded L'Heureux. It weighed anchor and sailed for France the next day. The Young Pretender's ambitions had been destroyed.

He landed in Brittany nine days later and was given the brief hospitality of the French Court, until the peace of Aix-la-Chapelle (1748) caused his forcible expulsion from France. He made two or three secret visits to London between 1750 and 1760, then assumed the title of Charles III of Great Britain and retired to Florence. He spent the rest of his life in fruitless intrigue. He married Louisa, Countess of Albany, in 1772, but the marriage was later dissolved. His daughter, Charlotte (1753 - 1789), by his mistress Clementine Walkinshaw, he had created Duchess of Albany. He died in Rome and was buried at Frascati, later reburied in St Peter's.

In July 1997 Lord Lester of Herne Hill, QC, was successful, after trying for thirty years, in persuading the Government to consider a new Bill of Rights, the first in Britain since the Glorious Revolution. It is hoped that the consequences of this Bill will not result in a series of events such as The Fifteen and The Forty-five, and that it will be relevant to ordinary people.

An Teallach

ELEVENTH STAGE:
Loch an Nid to Corrie Hallie (Dundonnell)
13 kilometres, 8.1 miles

In comparison with the tenth stage, this is quite straightforward, both navigationally and on the ground. The first five kilometres follow a reasonably defined path of variable quality. The remainder is on an engineered track, suitable for four-wheel drive vehicles, albeit rough in places.

Although in spectacular scenery, it may seem less varied than Stage Ten. An Teallach dominates. As you proceed north from Loch an Nid, its eastern spurs emerge and by the time you reach the track the whole ridge, with its eleven jagged peaks, is visible. Usually wreathed in smoke-like mists, from which it gets its name The Forge, this range, at 1062 metres, offers some of the best climbing in the Highlands. The traverse is

ELEVENTH STAGE
Loch an Nid to Corrie Hallie (Dundonnell)

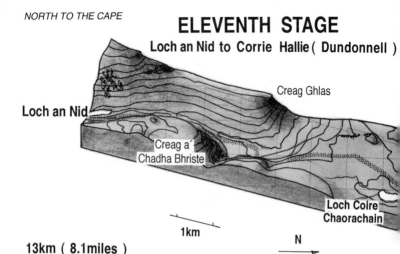

Creag Ghlas

Loch an Nid

Creag a'
Chadha Bhriste

Loch Coire
Chaorachain

1km

N

13km (8.1miles)

spectacular in winter, but is only for experienced climbers. It is much easier in summer, although a rope should still be carried to use if necessary. Whatever the season, the summit can be reached without any rock climbing.

As you climb out of Strath na Sealga up the steep track, your eyes will be drawn north-west to look along another glacial valley filled with water. This one is Loch na Sealga. The mountains to the south-west form the Fisherfield Forest, which vie with Knoydart to be the remotest part of the UK.

The summit of the pass seems even further away. After it, the descent into Gleann Chaorachain is very steep. The final two kilometres to the Dundonnell River and Corrie Hallie is a gentle drop through birchwoods and feels idyllic in comparison with the wild yompings of the last two days.

There are no facilities at Corrie Hallie itself, but the Dundonnell Hotel is three kilometres seaward on the road.

At this point you will have to decide whether to proceed on the definitive route or use the Ullapool Loop Variants (12 and 13). These will llow you to restock with provisions and enjoy the high life of the village or a break in the trek. We always enjoy our stays in Ullapool and can recommend it.

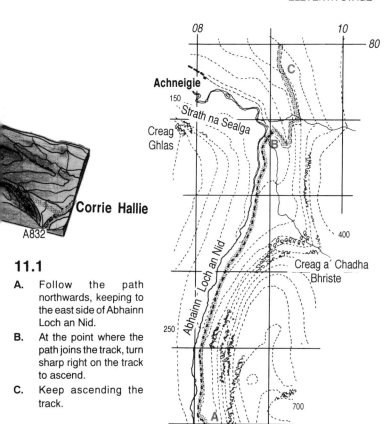

Map 11.1

11.1

A. Follow the path northwards, keeping to the east side of Abhainn Loch an Nid.

B. At the point where the path joins the track, turn sharp right on the track to ascend.

C. Keep ascending the track.

11.2

A. Follow the track.

B. Descend into Gleann Chaorachain.

C. Turn left at the A832.

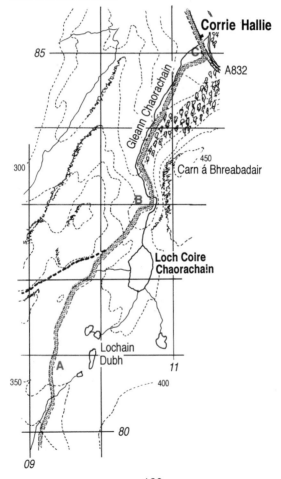

HAGGIS, NEEPS-AN' TATTIES

The twelve days of Christmas begin with the Feast of the Nativity on 25 December, and end with Epiphany on 6 January. In Scotland, two further celebrations enjoy equal or even greater public prominence around the turn of the year: Hogmanay, on 31 December, and Burns Night on 25 January.

New Year's Day was a Scottish public holiday, long before the rest of Britain adopted it in 1972. Hogmanay is said to be named after the French custom of *aguillanneuf*, 'a gift at the new year'. Many Hogmanay customs, notably that of first-footing, have their roots in Christmas or Hallowe'en. To be a first-foot, one must be male and dark haired. To be female or light haired, or even worse red haired, is seen as very bad luck. The first-footer must cross the threshold of a home after the stroke of midnight on New Year's Eve bearing gifts such as fuel, usually a piece of coal; food, usually oatcakes; and, almost invariably, whisky. In return for these tokens of good luck, the householder is expected to offer a dram, or two, or three.

Another tradition, practised in some Scottish towns and on the Borders, is that of 'burning the old year out'. This has its origins in old Norse and Anglo-Saxon fire-worship. After festivities around a communal bonfire, guests set out first-footing around the neighbourhood.

Whether the old year is burned out or not, the celebration of Hogmanay is notable for the consumption of copious quantities of food and drink; especially the Haggis. This celebrated dish features even more prominently when Robert Burns' birthday is marked throughout Scotland, and by Scots around the world, on 25 January. The traditional Burns Supper is followed by speeches, songs, recitations and sometimes Scottish dancing. It was inaugurated in Greenock in 1802, when the first Burns Club was started by a group of the poets' friends. In those days the *pièce de résistance* at the banquet was a sheep's head, eventually superseded by a Haggis.

The Supper usually starts with the 'Selkirk Grace'. Although it is not listed in some Complete Works of Robert Burns, it is usually attributed to him:

> Some hae meat, and canna eat,
> And some wad eat that want it,
> But we hae meat and we can eat,
> And sae the Lord be thank it.

A flourish on the bagpipe heralds the arrival of the Haggis, which is carried in procession around the room and placed before the chairman. He then calls on someone to address the Haggis. There follows a recitation of several verses of the Burns poem *To A Haggis*, the first verse being:

> Fair fa' your honest, sousie face,
> Great chieften o' the puddin-race.
> Aboon then a' ye tak your place,
> Painch, tripe, or thairm:
> Weel are ye wordy of a *grace*
> As lang's my arm.

The Haggis is then ceremoniously cut into and served. Many toasts and speeches follow, including the loyal toast, one to the immortal memory of Burns, one to 'oor land' and another to 'the lasses', the latter reflecting the poet's fondness for women. At some stage, the *Flower of Scotland*, also known as the Scottish Anthem, is sung. This is the name given to Scots who stood against the English to defend their homeland and send the Sassenachs back to England 'Tae think again'. A typical Burns Night Supper menu might be:

> Cock-a-Leekie
> Salmon
> Haggis, Neeps an' Tatties
> Roast Beef
> Atholl Brose Pudding
> Scottish Cheeses

Those of you who enjoy cooking may wish to prepare your own Haggis. This is what you must do:
Take a sheep's stomach bag and wash thoroughly in cold water. Turn it inside out, scald it and thoroughly scrape the surface with a knife. Soak overnight in cold salted water.

Take a sheep's pluck (heart, liver and lights — the tongue may also be added), and clean thoroughly. Make cuts in the liver and heart to let out the blood and boil the whole in salted water, letting the windpipe hang over the side into a bowl to collect the blood which will escape from the lungs. Cook for about one-and-a-half hours. Cool, then, after trimming away the skin, gristle and black looking bits, mince finely the heart, half the liver and all the lights. Add a pound of shredded minced beef suet, the other half of the liver, chopped, and three large onions, peeled, scalded and minced. Add a breakfast-cupful of pinhead oatmeal, toasted to a light-brown colour. Season to taste and mix well.

With the rough surface of the bag on the outside, stuff with the minced meat mixture after softening with about a half litre of the liquor in which the pluck was boiled. Fill the bag just over half full to allow for swelling of the contents, add a little vinegar, press out the air and sew up the bag with a trussing needle and fine string. Prick the bag in several places with a needle and, if the bag is thin, tie it in a cloth. Place the bag on an enamel dish, to prevent it sticking to the pan, and boil for about three hours. Serve hot with bashed neeps (mashed turnips) and chappit tatties (mashed potatoes). Several drams of single malt whisky should accompany the eating of this dish.

You may find that the ingredients are difficult to obtain, unless you know a 'real' butcher. Or, you may not feel adventurous enough to embark on making this dish, but all is not lost. You can buy perfectly good ready-made Haggis in Scotland and in many butchers shops and supermarkets in England.

The Ferryboat Inn

TWELFTH STAGE:
Corrie Hallie to Inverlael (Ullapool).
(See Variants 12 & 13)
10.2 kilometres, 6.3 miles

If, at the end of Stage Eleven, you were attracted by the bright lights of Ullapool, this stage and the next one will not feature in your itinerary. It is a short stage, but very welcome after the long, arduous journey from Kinlochewe to Corrie Hallie and before the lengthy crossing from Inverlael to Oykel Bridge.

The climb from the Dundonnell River is steep and rough, but not very long. At first, the views are constrained by the high sides of the glen. But, after about 100 metres, the going becomes easier and the way more gentle, both in terms of steepness and of ground work. Once the enclosed land is left behind there is open moorland which rises, with a defined path, on the southern flank of Meall a' Chairn; a mere 400 metres but the highest point of this stage.

We are not anglers ourselves, but we reckon that the many lochs and lochans around here must be a paradise for those who are. Our route passes around one of the larger ones (Loch an Tiompain) which, on a warm day, provides a haven of tranquillity. Regrettably, when we were there the day was grey and damp so we did not pause to take in the scene.

About half a kilometre beyond Loch an Tiompain, the descent begins and a good length of Strath More (the valley carrying the River Broom) is seen both north and south. Forward (ESE) Beinn Dearg (1,084 metres) is visible on a clear day some 10 kilometres away.

The descent is very steep initially and in places is slippery when wet, but the path is clear. Lower down it is undefined, but should present no problems.

From Croftown to the A835, you cross yet another alluvial flat before plodding northwards on the road. There is vehicular access to Croftown if you are being supported in this way.

There are no shops at all, but there is B & B accommodation about one kilometre along the minor road leading to Letters on the west side of Loch Broom.

TWELFTH STAGE

Corrie Hallie (Dundonnell) to Inverlael (Ullapool)

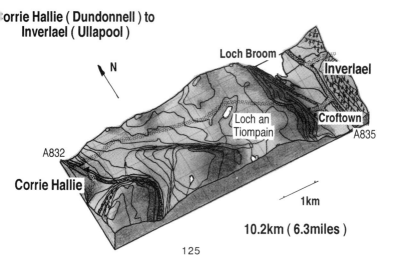

10.2km (6.3miles)

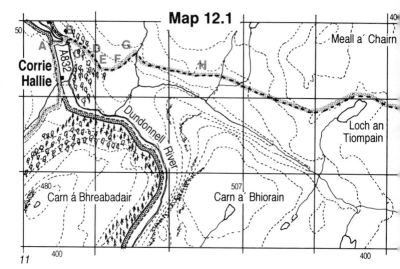

12.1

A. Turn right on the metalled road to cross the bridge over the Dundonnell River.

B. Immediately after the bridge, pass through the gate on your right. Then turn left to leave the track and ascend the hillside. No path.

C. Gradually turn SE as you ascend through the trees. The ill-defined formal path will be found.

D. Follow the path ascending through the wood.

E. Pass through a gate in the fence on leaving the wood.

F. Path defined. Another fence and gate.

G. At the head of the waterfall, cross the burn. (The crossing could be dangerous if the burn is in spate, as a slip might result in a fall over the cascade. You may have to find a higher crossing point.)

H. The path is now defined with occasional cairns. Gates in fences identify the route.

I. The path becomes undefined on the descent. Keep SE.

J. Make for the S (upper) end of the small plantation.

K. Turn sharp left (NNE) and keep the trees on your right. The descent is very rough.

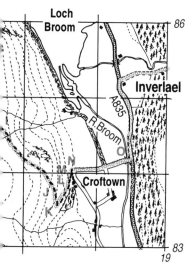

L. Leave the trees and keep the cottages away on your right.

M. At the end of the row of cottages, when clear of the bushes, turn right to descend. Then turn right again to make for and pass through the small gate which seems to give access to the cottage gardens. It doesn't. The way is now obvious and the access way to the dwellings is reached.

N. Make for the lane, then keep ahead to the A835.

O. Turn left at the road and proceed towards Ullapool for about 1 kilometre.

Variant 12: **Corrie Hallie to Ullapool**
9.5 kilometres, 5.9 miles
OS Landranger 19. Gairloch and Ullapool Area

This is the route you will take if you choose to visit Ullapool. Most of the way is on a metalled lane, but the scenery provides some compensation. You will need to use the foot passenger ferry across Loch Broom. It is operated from the hotel at Allt na h'Airbhe, where arrangements for the crossing can be made. We found this hotel too expensive for our tastes, but if you wish to indulge yourself you would be wise to make advance arrangements as it is often booked up months ahead.

From Corrie Hallie, follow the definitive route to cross the Dundonnell River.

At -

114856 Do NOT go through the gate, but keep on the lane. Follow it to the bealach at -

100919 Join the path and descend NNE to the hotel and the ferry.

See Feature "Ullapool".

ULLAPOOL

By the time you get to the A837 (Destitution Road) at Corrie Hallie, marking the end of Stage Eleven, you will have walked in excess of 150 kilometres. A few more kilometres away lies the village of Ullapool. It has several hotels, many B & Bs, guesthouses, a Youth Hostel, a camping site, restaurants, pubs galore, shops, a bank and a Tourist Information Centre. It even has its own radio station. In case you are attracted by the delights of this village, we offer in the Appendix a suggested route there, plus a way of rejoining the definitive walk.

And, after the two-day journey from Kinlochewe, you may wish to whet your appetite for dry beds by walking a few extra kilometres and staying the night at Dundonnell at the head of Loch Broom. It has an hotel plus two or three bunkhouses, a petrol station, but no shop. If you do this, you will have to return to Corrie Hallie to continue your walk.

From Corrie Hallie, you will make your way to the small, but exclusive, hotel and restaurant at Allt na h'Airbhe, Alt-na Harrie, or Altnaharrie as it is variously known. This famous, seriously expensive, establishment, allegedly one of the best, if not the best, in the Western Highlands, gets booked up sometimes months in advance. Of greatest advantage to the walker, is the fact that there is a ferry service from the hotel to Ullapool.

When you disembark from the (small) ferry, opposite the Ferry Boat Inn, be careful not to slip on the stony beach in your eagerness to sample the urban pleasures awaiting you.

Over 3,000 years ago, Neolithic hunter-gatherers eked out a precarious living among the bears, wolves and wild boars which inhabited the forests along the coastline of North-west Ross. Small communities developed near the shoreline. Plentiful supplies of shellfish were supplemented by vegetables from primitive smallholdings.

Irish monks brought Christianity

Lying in the Bath

I lie in my bath
A cup or glass of something
*   at arm's reach*
Raise my feet out of the suds
And rest them on the rim;
Drink a toast to my toes
To my heels, to my ankles
And
When they are in sight
To my boots

To my Boots and my Feet
An essential pair of couplings
On a well-walked day

to the area in the seventh century. In their wake came the feared Vikings from their settlements in Orkney and Shetland. The rugged coastline, with its many fiord-like lochs, may have reminded them of their homelands, for many of them settled in the area. Some place names serve as reminders of their influence over several centuries. Gruinard, meaning 'shallow fiord', derives from their 'grunna fiord' and Ullapool, meaning 'Ulli's steading', derives from 'Ullibolstode'.

In the early thirteenth century, power shifted to the Scottish clans. Loch Broom is nearly 34 kilometres long, the longest sea loch in the North-west Highlands, and Inverlael, at its head, became the most important village in the Lochbroom district. The land around became Clan Donald country. Dundonnell comes from this period and derives from 'Dun Dohmnull', 'the fort of Donald'. The district of Lochbroom was ruled by the MacDonalds of Lochalsh until 1518, when MacDonald of Glengarry inherited one half and Mackenzie of Kintail the other. Following many years of feuding between these two families, the Mackenzies finally acquired the whole of North-west Ross. They remained in control until Bonnie Prince Charlie's ignominious defeat at Culloden in 1746, after which the land was forfeit.

From then on, life became increasingly difficult. Many were ousted in the dreaded Clearances, to make way for sheep. Poverty gripped all who remained, until 1788, which proved to be a turning point.

The committee of The British Society for Extending the Fisheries and Improving the Sea Coasts of This Kingdom of Great Britain (unbelievably, that was the official name of 'The British Fisheries Society')

Boots

Boots, ah, boots!
Couldn't they tell a long, long tale
Did the Wordsworths wear wellies
Mid primroses pale?
Did they gently scrape the mud
From interstices of the sole?
Had they mugger hobs and clinkers
Wear-and-tearings to control
Or tricounis, three-in-ones?
Had the cobblers of Northampton
Invented bellow-tongues?

Oh, choose wisely, my fair daughter
On your first, untrodden ways
Buy them slowly, wear them in
For they hold the key to treasures
Where the open roads begin

decided that Ullapool should become one of its fishing stations. On 13 June 1788, the good ship Gilmorton sailed into Loch Broom, with 55 passengers: 1 Blacksmith, 1 Cooper, 1 Fish Curer, 1 Heckler, 2 Joiners, 7 Masons, 1 Netmaker, 1 Slater and their families. These artisans were to build streets, houses and shops, the nucleus of a new village. Problems developed with the foundations of the pier in 1790, but rescue was at hand. Engineer Thomas Telford, no less, was appointed Surveyor of Buildings and became responsible for much of Ullapool's grid layout and architecture.

In 1880, Ullapool fell on evil times, with a rapid decline in the herring industry. The local economy faced virtual collapse. Only the budding tourist industry, with visitors travelling by coach from Strathpeffer on the east coast and by steamer from Glasgow, provided the village with hope for the future.

Nowadays Ullapool thrives on a combination of fishing (lobsters and prawns), servicing the ferry to Stornoway in the Outer Hebrides and tourism. It has boat cruises, a pipe band, a leisure centre and swimming pool, a wildlife hospital, an angling club, sites of archaeological interest including a prehistoric settlement, a museum with Visitor Centre and a Tourist Information Centre. It also has a clock, some Klondikers and a Community Radio Station.

The square, cast iron timepiece, known locally as the Fowler Memorial Clock, stands in Quay Street and is reputedly the most photographed clock in the Highlands. It was erected in 1899 in memory of Sir John Fowler and his family. John Fowler (1817 - 1898) was born in Wadsley Hall, Ecclesfield near Sheffield. From his youth he was involved in railway construction, including the London Metropolitan Railway and Victoria Station. He instigated a project to build a Garve and Ullapool Railway, but it came to nothing. He designed the Pimlico Railway bridge and, with Sir Benjamin Baker, the Forth Railway bridge. Sir John and his family lived at Braemore House, Braemore Junction near Corrieshalloch Gorge. The Fowlers presented the clock to the village in 1922, together with £100 to invest for maintenance purposes. There are plaques on its pedestal with dedicatory inscriptions to various members of the family. The clock was wound by hand until 1995, when an electric motor was fitted.

Fishing has played an important role in the economy of the village for 200 years, but with alternating periods of glut and dearth. When herring was plentiful, the industry prospered. When herring failed, the industry fell into decline and the villagers had to look elsewhere for an income. After World War II, fishing techniques improved through technological change and the increased size of boats. But again the boom did not last. In the late 60s, low draft Scandinavian 'Klondikers' appeared in Loch Broom, so called after the enormous influx of treasure hunters to the Klondike in 1896. The treasure this time was herring. They employed local men to freeze the fish caught by east coast boats. The fish was then taken to ports around the world. Herring again declined in 1975 but news of the nutritional value of mackerel brought them to the fore. The 'Klondikers' struck again. Loch Broom was filled with anything up to 70 Eastern Bloc factory ships. Sometimes, Nigerian, Irish, French and even Japanese 'Klondikers' also swelled the numbers of ships at anchor. Ullapool prospered again, busy by day and magical at night, with the dipping, bobbing mast head and working lights and their shimmering reflections. Today, the appearance of the floating factories is sporadic and Ullapool's fishing fleet now numbers only about a dozen boats.

Lochbroom FM started life in a distinctive blue corrugated iron shack, with its back to the sea, across the road from the bank in Argyle Street. A community radio station, serving the Ullapool and Achiltibuie areas, it first broadcast in the summer of 1995 on a frequency of 105.4 FM. It is run entirely by volunteers, broadcasting at breakfast time and in the evenings. Between times, Virgin Radio is re-broadcast on its frequency. The breakfast show includes local weather, what's on, road reports, other tourist information and, most importantly, a 'midgie' count. Now transmitting on a frequency of 102.2 FM it is currently located in the Industrial Estate east of Mill Street and visitors are welcome, so why not pop in?

If you visit Ullapool, we are sure that you will enjoy the experience, but all good things must come to an end. It is time now to depart. So, pack your rucksack and stride out ever-northwards. The Cape beckons you.

In case you are curious, 'Destitution Road' is so called because, in common with other similar roads, it was built in 1851 to give work to starving men during the potato famine. A 'Heckler' prepared the hemp for net making. (We can find no connection between this meaning and the usually accepted meaning of the word 'heckle').

Eagle

*Close to the sun
in lonely lands*
(Tennyson)

THIRTEENTH STAGE:
Inverlael to Knockdamph (See Variants 12 & 13)
16.8 kilometres, 10.4 miles

This stage, together with that immediately following, connects the community at Inverlael on the A835 with that at Oykel Bridge on the A837; a total distance of 29.8 kilometres, 18.5 miles. There is no habitation between, so a camp is necessary unless you are very fit and can convert the two stages into one.

The first few kilometres run beside the River Lael on forest roads. Just after entering the forest area, cross the river on two bridges in tandem. At

Loch a´
Ghille

Inverlael

132

this point the Lael is divided by a rocky island springing out of a deep gorge. Do look into the two branches of the gorge and see the turbulent river. A kilometre-and-a-half beyond the bridges, the route follows the forest road as it turns north-east to follow a tributary of the Lael. Soon, you ascend steeply on a very rough, ill-defined path, through the forest. When we were there, it had been recently harvested.

After leaving the forest area the ascent continues on what must be a recently made track, as OS shows a path. The ascent is steep, since you leave the Lael 100 metres or so above sea level and reach 450 metres within about two kilometres. At this point, we were denied what must be fine views since there was heavy cloud and use of the compass was necessary. From OS, we conclude that, as you look back WNW from the higher part of the climb, you will see over the forest and Strath More to Carn a' Bhiorain and possibly the route of the previous stage.

Ahead, at the end of the track, you will have to ford a burn and cross a small section of peat bog to reach higher ground NE. We tried to avoid a further ascent and found ourselves

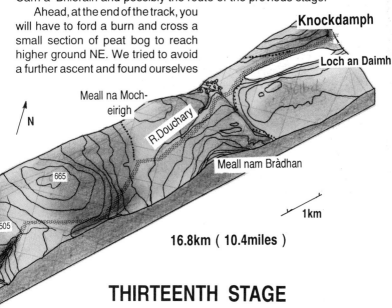

Knockdamph

Loch an Daimh

Meall na Moch-eirigh

R.Douchary

Meall nam Bràdhan

N

665

505

1km

16.8km (10.4miles)

THIRTEENTH STAGE

Inverlael to Knockdamph

133

floundering in the peat, jumping water courses and tending to lose our sense of direction because of cloud. Do NOT get bogged down — make for higher ground.

The descent into Glen Douchary is very rough and slow, but looking ahead you should see the River Douchary and, in due course, the ruins of the settlement of Douchary. (OS does not indicate the ruins, although they do exist on the ground.)

We strongly recommend your crossing the River Douchary as soon as you can (see navigation notes), as a crossing lower down will be difficult, if not impossible, as it rushes down a gorge. Around the ruins, the glen is more like a strath and the river is broad and shallow. We were able to wade across without the water overtopping our boots.

Whilst in the strath, if you look SE up Gleann a' Chadha Dheirg (beyond the range of our maps) you can see the rocky cliffs at Cadha Dearg some four or five kilometres away.

As you descend Glen Douchary, make sure you are on the E side of the river. A path is shown on OS, but for practical purposes it is non-existent, making the going very rough. The consolation lies in the scenery, made great by the tumbling river on your left.

As the river turns W to pass down Glen Achall and on to the sea near Ullapool, our route turns ENE to make for the SW shore of Loch an Daimh less than one kilometre away. In due course, this loch drains NE into the River Oykel and on to the North Sea at Dornach Firth. You are, then, at the watershed of this wee part of Scotland. The walk along the NW shore of Loch an Daimh is straightforward except that you may find yourself splashing in the water, occasionally seeing the remains of the original path.

The last kilometre to Knockdamph is on a well-maintained track.

If you choose to use the bothy, we trust you to follow the rules.

13.1

A. Turn right, to leave the A835 through the gate between the 'phone box and the cottage.

B. Proceed on the track, and pass through the gate into the forest area.

C. Bear left and cross the two bridges which span deep gorges through which

Map 13.1

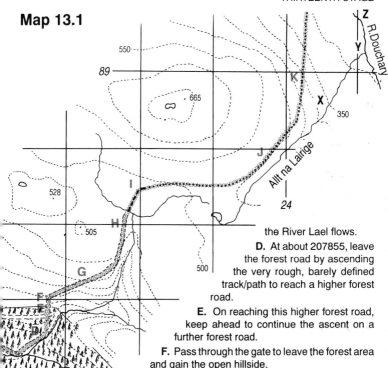

the River Lael flows.

D. At about 207855, leave the forest road by ascending the very rough, barely defined track/path to reach a higher forest road.

E. On reaching this higher forest road, keep ahead to continue the ascent on a further forest road.

F. Pass through the gate to leave the forest area and gain the open hillside.

G. Continue on this track until it ends at the junction of two burns (218872) at —

H. Beyond here, the ground is very difficult peat bog. To avoid this as much as possible, continue NNE for about 400 metres to higher ground before turning E at —

I. 220875. Then walk E on the contour for about one kilometre and wheel round NE keeping on the contour. No path.

J. Descend parallel with the Allt na Lairige.

K. When the remains of the settlement at Douchary (244902, not on OS) appear to the N, make your way to them. The ground is rough, so there may be advantage in following the Allt na Lairige to its junction with the River Douchary and then following the latter downstream (N). Cross the river when you can (XYZ, not researched).

13.2

A. Cross the River Douchary as soon as practicable (we crossed at 247905). If you follow OS on the W side of the river and try to cross at 250911, you will probably find it very difficult.

B. Follow the E side of the river on the ill-defined path, which is very rough and hence slow.

C. Do NOT descend into the gorge, but turn NE. There is no path on the very rough grass. Descend and then ascend to cross the Allt nan Caorach.

D. Keep ENE. No path and rough. Make for the SW end of Loch an Daimh at —

E. Keep as close to the shore of the loch as possible.

F. Pass the boat house and continue on the shore of the loch. No properly defined path except for a few remnants.

G. Join the track and continue NE.

H. Bothy at Knockdamph.

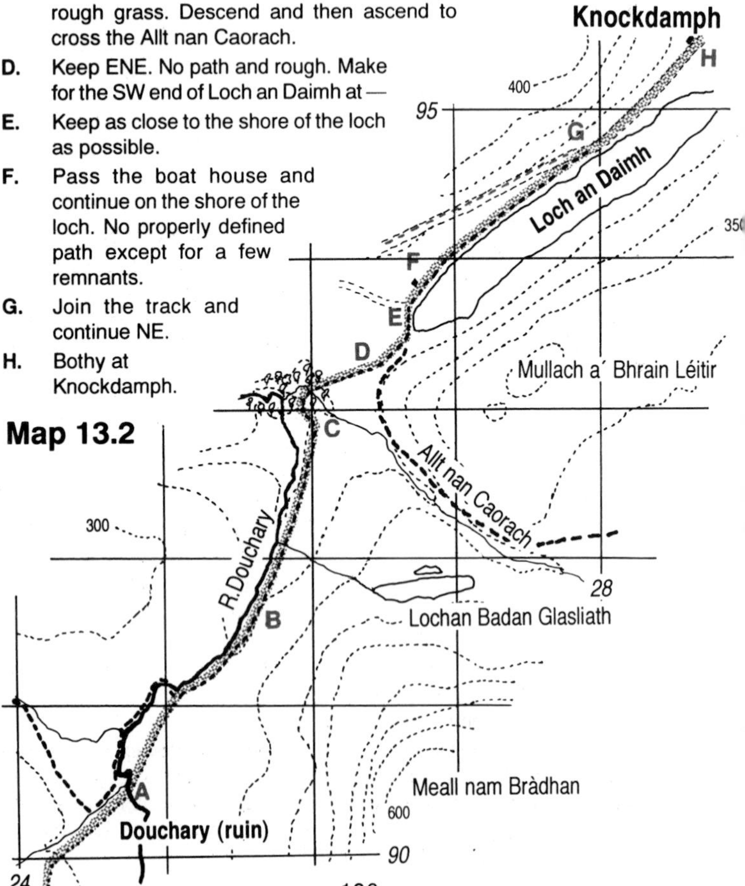

Map 13.2

Knockdamph

Loch an Daimh

Mullach a' Bhrain Léitir

Allt nan Caorach

R.Douchary

Lochan Badan Glasliath

Meall nam Bràdhan

Douchary (ruin)

300

400

350

95

28

90

24

> ## *Variant 13:* **Ullapool to Knockdamph**
> 18.2 kilometres, 11.3 miles
> OS Landranger 19. Gairloch and Ullapool Area
> OS Landranger 20. Ben Dearg & surrounding area

If you visit Ullapool you will have to return to the definitive route, hence the following variant. You will need provisions for at least eight days. The route is navigationally simple, but on a well-made track which makes the ground work rather uninteresting. The scenery changes but slowly, and is in our view not as varied as on the definitive route.

Leave Ullapool northwards on the A835. At —

129949   just before the main road crosses the Ullapool River, turn right and follow the track (estate road) passing Loch Achall on your right and Rhidorroch House on your left. At—

236937   pass East Rhidorroch Lodge on your right. At —

250932   the track turns NE. Keep ahead at

260938   OS shows the track becoming a path, but we recall it continuing as a track.

278947   Loch an Daimh is on your right. Join the definitive route.

CALMAC

The Viking Age proper extended from the eighth to the eleventh century, but it is known that these bold Scandinavians ventured abroad much earlier. Historians have authenticated raids on the Hebrides and the Donegal Coast as early as the seventh century. The warriors ranged far and wide, covering the coasts of most North and West European countries, although the main areas of concentration were the Low Countries, Western France, Ireland and Great Britain. The first recorded raid on England occurred as far south as Wessex, in 789.

The Vikings had a reputation for being fierce and cruel, with rape and pillage their received modus operandi. In low, single-decked long ships, propelled by oar and square sail, these disciplined fighting men wreaked havoc wherever they landed, leaving behind a wake of blood and destruction. They rounded Cape Wrath in 875, to ransack both the West Coast of Scotland and the Hebrides. Then, King Harald Fairhair of

Norway established his suzerainty over the vanquished Hebridean territories. He granted them to the Jarls of Sudreyar, better known as the Lords of the Isles, singularly immortalised by Sir Walter Scott's ballad written in 1815. The Lords intermittently remained Norwegian vassals until the 1266 Treaty of Perth, when King Magnus Hakonarson of Norway surrendered his claims. The many Norse place names in the Highlands and Islands remain testimony to the half-millennium of Viking rule.

The islands around Scotland are no longer visited by the unwelcome ships of conquering warriors, but by the welcome ships of Caledonian MacBrayne. During your walk you will never be far from the coast, and it is possible that, given good weather and a high vantage point, you will see these vessels plying between the mainland and the islands. If you visit Ullapool, you cannot fail to notice the presence of the Ullapool - Stornaway ferry service.

The company's origins go back many years. Founder David MacBrayne operated ferry services around the West Coast from 1851, and the Caledonian Steam Packet Company, formed in 1889, provided services on the Firth of Clyde. MacBrayne was jointly owned by a railway company and Coastlines Ltd. Caledonian was wholly railway-owned; both were taken over by the Scottish Transport Group in 1969 and named Caledonian MacBrayne on 1 January 1973. They became the direct responsibility of the Secretary of State for Scotland in 1990.

The company currently operates ferries to 23 islands, from the five minute shuttle service across the Kyles of Bute to the seven-and-a-quarter hour voyage from Oban, via Barra, to Lochboisdale in South Uist. The fleet of more than 30 vessels ranges from the small 'island' class ferries, carrying 50 passengers and 6 cars, to the largest, capable of carrying up to 1,000 people and 120 cars. After prolonged, sometimes heated, 'discussions' with sabbatarians, the operators now provide sailings seven days a week. The larger vessels have self-service restaurants, bars and the ubiquitous souvenir shops. Some also have cabin accommodation. In addition to the regular ferry services CalMac, as it is affectionately known, offers day cruises in season and special events, such as 'Dine Aboard Cruises' complete with silver service.

As well as providing services for tourists, eager to experience the 'sea roads to the Isles', the company provides vital lifelines to the remote populations. Carrying commuters, essential supplies, and some not so essential, the ferries also convey produce and livestock to mainland markets.

As one might expect, the Islanders have a love-hate relationship with CalMac. The company was threatened with privatisation in 1988 and, in particular, the hiving off of the profitable Clyde routes, including Arran, from the rest of the the Western Isles Services. It was a pleasant surprise, not least to CalMac and friends, when almost 100% of Arran residents were first to register their objections to the proposed changes. The plans were put 'on ice'.

Most companies have their critics, and CalMac is no exception. In 1990 they delayed one of their sailings from Mull, with its inadequate medical facilities, to take on board an expectant mother. A coach courier wrote to *The Oban Times* complaining bitterly because his passengers were late for dinner at their Oban hotel, precipitating lengthy correspondence. One suspects that the Highlanders and Islanders would rather just miss a boat than not have one at all, although CalMac claims to complete at least 95% of its sailings on time.

Whether you wish to visit Barra or Berneray, Coll or Colonsay, Scalpay or Skye, Rum, Eigg or Muck, Caledonian MacBrayne will get you there. For, as a modern parody on Psalm 24, A Psalm for David, puts it:

> "The earth belongs unto the Lord,
> and all that it contains,
> except for the Clyde and Western Isles
> They're Caledonian MacBrayne's"

The Monarch of the Glen - Apologies to Landseer

FOURTEENTH STAGE:
Knockdamph to Oykel Bridge
13 kilometres, 8.1 miles

Navigationally, this stage is very straightforward. The only problem is tactical, namely the crossing of the Abhainn Poiblidh, since you might have to wade. The whole way follows well-defined tracks, initially on open moorland but later and lower through a forest. At 13 kilometres it is not very long, by contrast with the previous stage.

FOURTEENTH STAGE

Knockdamph to Oykel Bridge

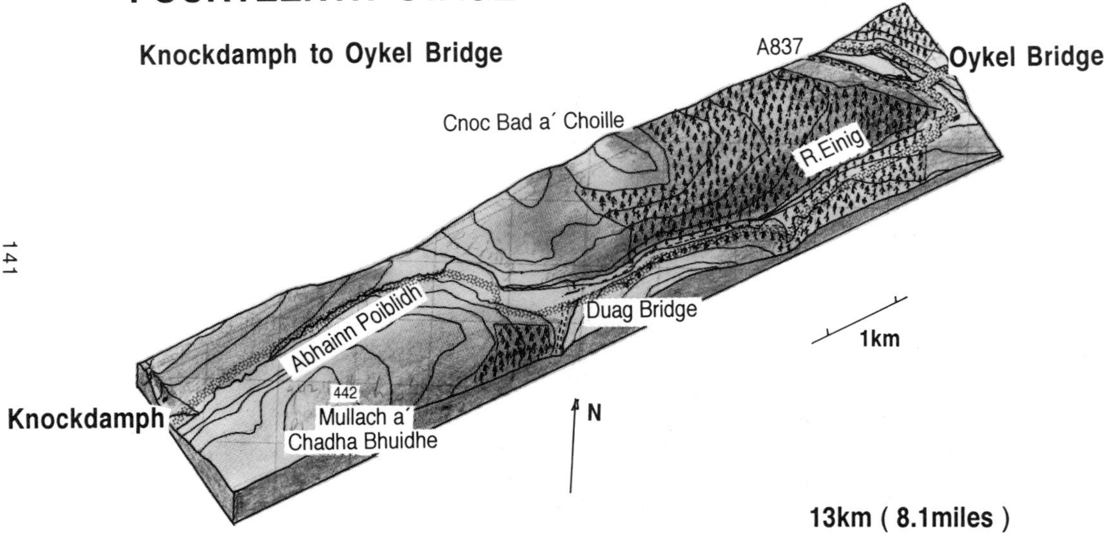

Oykel Bridge

A837

R.Einig

Cnoc Bad a´ Choille

Duag Bridge

N

Abhainn Poiblidh

442

Mullach a´
Chadha Bhuidhe

Knockdamph

1km

13km (8.1miles)

We cannot say the scenery is special. However we conclude that it is especial angling country, judged by the number of fishermen seen and the number of empty cars parked a short walk from the rivers.

It is, perhaps, fatuous to say that this is forest country, but often forests provide scenic variety; more importantly they present a fascinating habitat for wildlife. If you observe the micro-landscapes closely there is a lot to see in them. Remember too, that most of Scotland was covered in trees until our forbears removed them; albeit, the character of the aboriginal forests was different.

There is an hotel at Oykel Bridge on the A837, which may provide meals for non-residents. There are a few cottages, but there is no shop.

14.1

A.   Continue on the well-defined track (shown on OS as a path).

B.   Crossing the Abhainn Poiblidh could be difficult when in spate. You may have to wade or find a crossing point elsewhere, although this could also be difficult.

C.   Defined track.

D.   Join the main track beside the Abhainn Dubhag, turning left then right to cross Duag Bridge.

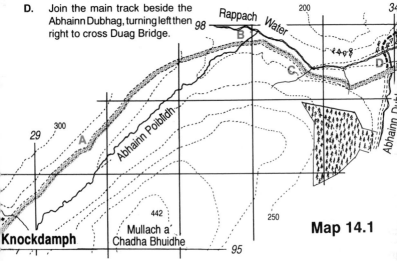

Map 14.1

14.2

A. OS shows two forward routes. The upper route proceeds outside the forest and the lower goes through the forest near the River Einig. Arbitrarily, we chose the lower route. However, you may wish to use the upper one which we have not researched.

B. Again, OS shows an upper and lower route. We chose the lower, shorter route, and have not researched the upper one.

C. Turn left, then right to cross the bridge over the River Einig.

D. At the A837, turn right over the old bridge and then left into the forest road.

E. If the gate is closed, use the stile over the fence a few metres to the left. (There is a footpath alongside the River Oykel, which affords spectacular views of the river racing down a small gorge. However, there is no way through to the defined route.)

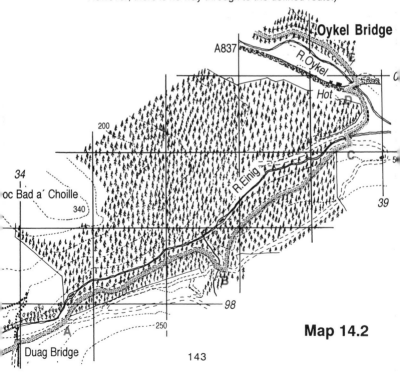

Map 14.2

143

What?

I said put aside your camera and come here!

What?

Come and stand!

By this running, rushing river
With its peaty, frothing contents
Like some madly fleeing beer
From a brewery

Hold tight onto the barrier
Lest these slackly bedded pebbles
And this mesmerising, all out-shouting
Rackety, riotous river pitches us up
Adrenaline first
To ride the dizzy zeniths of pure vertigo
Down, down, down, down, down
Into its now transparent, now flamboyant
Chaos of refractions
As it hurtles to the sea
With urgencies of
Fresh water
To soften
The decongesting reek of shoreline seaweed
And temper
Neptune's salty beard

Sated by aquatic fears and fancies
They moved off
Just once more backward glancing
To watch the river make
Its lithesome, slithersome way
Along the glen

As the watery roar receded
Their ears retuned to birdsong
And the satin sounds of sheep
Uprooting grassy tresses

Then they turned back
To their cameras
And gathered up their gear

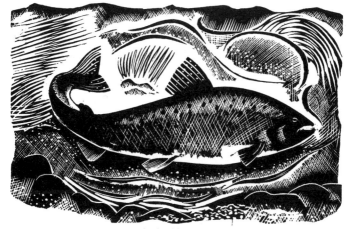

In the Maelstrom

FIFTEENTH STAGE:
Oykel Bridge to Loch Ailsh
13.1 kilometres, 8.1 miles

Except for a very awkward section of about half-a-kilometre rising over rough ground through dense trees, this is another straightforward stage both navigationally and on the ground. It ascends Glen Oykel beside the River Oykel on a forest/estate road for about nine kilometres, to reach a forest road higher up the glen. Just over three kilometres later, Loch Ailsh is reached.

The glen is quite wide and open (perhaps it should be called a strath?) and the surrounding hills are not very high so you get a 'big space' feeling. The river is obviously an angling river (salmon perhaps), and the peace and remoteness certainly must be attractive to those engaging in piscatorial pursuits.

At the time of research, the higher road offered pleasant views over the trees W & NW, while the background and middle distance is forest. NNW the massif of Breabeag can be seen, ten kilometres away.

If you wanted to avoid the said very difficult half-kilometre, you could walk up the road (A837); in which case, pass the hotel in a westerly direction on the road and keep walking. There is usually little traffic, except for the occasional articulated lorry. We wondered whether they were plying their way between the fishing villages of Kinlochbervie or Lochinver and the east coast at Bonar Bridge, for its easy access to the communications based on the A9 and the railway. After 12 kilometres, having passed Loch Craggie, an estate road goes off to the right, reaching Loch Ailsh after another three kilometres. There is a hut which provides a good navigation point (297083), indicating where to leave the road. This option increases the stage from 13.1 kilometres to about 15 kilometres.

There is no road access at the end of this Stage, although the estate road will provide emergency access.

FIFTEENTH STAGE

Oykel Bridge to Loch Ailsh

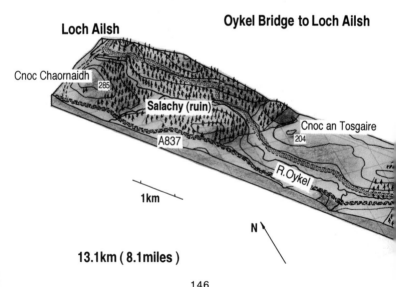

13.1km (8.1miles)

15.1

A. Continue on the well-maintained forest/estate road.

B. Leave the forest area.

C. Continue.

Map 15.1

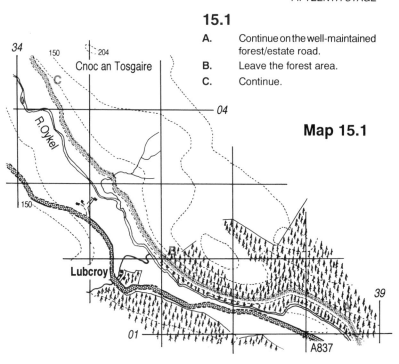

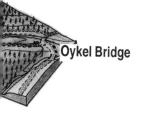

Oykel Bridge

15.2

A. Continue on the forest/estate road.

B. OS shows the road terminating here, but on the ground it continues to Salachy. Keep ahead.

C. At the end of the forest road, proceed on the ill-defined path through rough grass. Cross the boggy burn and go through the opening in the fence. The going is rough and the path non-existent. Turn N to leave the River Oykel and approach the ruins of Salachy. With the ruins on your left, pass through a 'gate opening' towards the trees.

Cross the burn and ascend on its W bank. The going is very rough and in places you may have to enter the trees.

D. After rather less than half-a-kilometre above Salachy, you will reach a forest road. Turn left (NW).

(Our choice of the W bank of the burn to ascend was arbitrary. The E bank

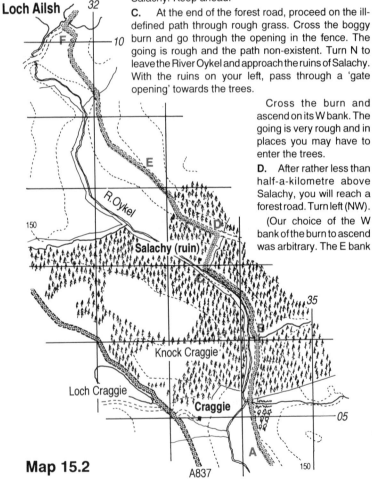

Map 15.2

148

may also be possible, and there is a bridge across the burn at the road. There may be other ways, but they are not apparent. Whichever way you use, reach the forest road and turn left.)

E.   Continue on the forest road to the junction on the shore of Loch Ailsh at:

F.   Turn right towards Benmore Lodge.

CROFTS AND CLEARANCES

Travellers in the Highlands and Islands of Scotland will see many crofts. Often in idyllic surroundings, the cottages, sometimes thatched and sometimes with a 'tin' roof, offer the casual visitor an image of tranquillity with the sheltering glens providing a good life of self sufficiency. There is little reality in this image. Life on crofts has always been hard and seldom materially rewarding.

Three hundred years ago, prior to the establishment of crofts, one third of Scotland's population lived in the Highlands. Then, the islands and glens were bustling, lively places. The Chief looked on his clan as a loyal family. He divided and leased his lands to tacksmen, often close relatives, who were responsible for the day-to-day running of the estate. The tacksmen rented the land to tenant farmers who, in turn, employed cottars to operate the runrig system of cultivation for them. Runrigs were narrow strips of land, which were balloted for each year so that everyone got a fair share of good and poor land. The cottars ploughed the fields, harvested the crops, herded the cattle and cut the peat. In return they received a roof over their head and a small patch of land on which to grow their own food. For part of the year members of the clan lived as farmers, but in the fighting season, usually summer, the tacksmen recruited them to follow their Chief into battle.

The Fifteen and the Forty-five Jacobite rebellions ended in the defeat of Bonnie Prince Charlie and his Gaelic supporters at Culloden in 1746. There followed a period of repression. Most of the inhabitants of Gaelic Scotland were punished, with many Jacobites being executed, imprisoned or banished. The King's soldiers roamed the Highlands, committing brutal crimes against the people. Laws were passed, forbidding ownership of any weapons and the playing of the bagpipe. One of the worst sanctions was the banning of the tartan and the kilt, and it was the loss of this symbol of clan loyalty that started the break-up of the clan system.

After the persecutions of 1746, change was inevitable in the Highlands. Landowners, many of them absentees, sought new ways of making money from their land. They experimented with crop rotation, land drainage, hardier animal breeds and farm machines. Modernisation meant supplying the needs of developing industries in the Lowlands and England. Cattle had traditionally been the major export. Now, two other valuable exports were to be discovered: kelp and sheep. Kelping led to the establishment of small individual holdings which became known as crofts, derived from the Gaelic *coirtean* meaning a small enclosed field.

Kelp making involved the burning of seaweed, the ash being used in the manufacture of soap and glass because of the high content of sodium, potassium and magnesium salts. This was a labour-intensive operation, since twenty tonnes of wrack were required to produce one tonne of ash. It was also seasonal work, the weed being gathered from the shore at low water in summer and brought to the shore to be reduced in peat-fired kilns. The kelpers were offered the inducement of a small strip of land for their own use and a share in common grazing, as well as a small wage. It was sheep, however, that brought tragedy upon tragedy to the Highlands.

As part of their search for new ways of making money, many landowners brought sheep onto their estates. The Cheviot sheep was introduced in large numbers. It produced better, more valuable wool than the smaller native sheep. In summer, the new sheep grazed on the hills. In winter they needed the shelter of the valleys where many farmers and cottars lived in small townships. The people were ejected in a heartless epic of greed and base thuggery, now known as the Clearances, to make way for ever increasing numbers of sheep.

Thus, the Lairds cleared their estates, particularly in Knoydart and Sutherland. Men, women, children, the sick and infirm were dispatched by the factors (Lairds' Agents) from their homes, which were then razed to the ground. Hill grazing areas were burnt so that there would be no food for the cattle. Between 1807 and 1821, at least 10,000 men, women and children (almost half the population) were evicted from their homes in Sutherland alone. A report by the Napier Commission of Enquiry in 1883 recorded that:

'There was no mercy shown to young or old. All had to clear away, and those who could not get their effects removed in time to a safe place, had them burnt before their eyes.'

One might imagine that the prospect of eviction would lead to large-scale rebellion. This never happened because of the ban on the ownership of weapons, and in many areas the Lairds enforced their will on the people by using soldiers and police. Nor did the Church help. Most Ministers were appointed by the Laird and so could not advise their flock to break the law and offer resistance against the horror encroaching upon their lives

During 1762 - 1886, hundreds of Clearances took place. With nowhere to live and, in many cases, no belongings, the people of the Highlands faced four options. They could go abroad, and many thousands travelled afar to such places as Canada, the USA, South Africa, Australia and New Zealand. Men could join the army, and the fact that members of the British army were allowed to wear the kilt encouraged many to take this step. They could move to the Lowlands of Scotland to cities such as Glasgow, where there was work to be found in textile mills, on the railways, in the coal mines and shipbuilding. Or, they could settle on the coast on the new crofts.

The crofts were often on inhospitable, rocky and infertile land. If the crofters managed to improve the land the landowners raised the rent. The crofts were also too small to feed a family and pay the rent, and crofters had to find other work. Some men managed to learn new skills and face the dangers of the sea to earn a living. Fishing was, however, unreliable, being dependent both on the weather and on a plentiful supply of fish; neither could be guaranteed. At first, many found that kelping provided an income, even though kelpers suffered acutely from physical exhaustion and rheumatism by being continuously wet. But the price of kelp fell after 1811 due to the importation of cheaper borilla from Spain. Over the next 20 years, the kelp industry became less profitable than sheep farming and, once again, the crofters and the cottars were ejected.

Another disaster occurred in 1846, when the potato harvest was struck by blight. The Highlanders' main crop and staple diet was ruined. Mass starvation was narrowly averted by Government help and the efforts of charities and even some landowners. The new 1845 Poor Law forced landlords to care for the poor on their lands, but the potato famine helped to convince landlords it would be better to evict people rather than support them. There is no doubt that many able and enterprising families were lost to the Highlands for ever. Then, slowly, the tide began to turn.

During the 1850s, cheaper imported wool made Highland sheep farms less profitable and many Lairds turned their land over to sporting pursuits. This time, the sheep were cleared. Fishing and deerstalking provided rich rewards for the landowners as shooters and fishermen flocked to this, now empty, land. The Highlands and Islands became a playground for the wealthy. Some crofters gained employment as gillies and stalkers, some, especially women, as servants. This meant that their crofts became neglected and the land less fertile. The crofters were still in a very precarious situation.

In the 1880s, desperate to keep what little they had, the crofters at long last rebelled against the landowners. Thousands joined Land Leagues, to campaign for changes in the land laws. They wanted to protect the Highland traditions and customs, and managed to get supporters elected to Parliament. Men and women fought side by side in clashes with police. Gunboats arrived with soldiers to keep the peace, but the campaign went on. Ronald MacLean, speaking on the Isle of Sky e in 1884 said:

"Your fathers kept quiet — quiet since the '45. Tell me what they gained by it? Still keep up your agitation; let your enemies see you are not afraid of police or military — your agitation must and will go on until your wrongs are righted."

In 1883, the Government had despatched Lord Napier to investigate the Highland problem. His report resulted in the Crofters Holding (Scotland) Act of 1886, protecting crofters from eviction and unfair rents. It did not return the land to the people, so they continued over the next 30 years to try and take back, piece by piece, small areas which they considered rightly theirs.

1897 saw more Government action to improve the lot of crofters. The Highland Congested Districts Board was formed and funds were made available for road construction, and for developing the fishery and tweed industries. It still did not return the land to the people.

There was more discontent after World War I and more land raids took place. In 1919, the Land Settlement (Scotland) Bill gave powers of compulsory purchase to the Board of Agriculture and provided loans to some tenants. Yet it still did not return the land to the people. By the early 1930s, life seemed to have gone out of the long struggle. Emigration to the big towns and overseas had drastically reduced the number of those still determined to live the life of a crofter.

World War II, with its need for coordinated effort by the whole nation, showed what could be achieved by machinery and fertilisers to bring poor hill land into cultivation. People were encouraged to stay on the land and subsidies were forthcoming. Small units were amalgamated into larger, more viable, ones and living standards rose. New jobs became available as road building, forestry and hydroelectric schemes proliferated.

In 1954, the Taylor Commission into crofting reported:

"The crofting system deserves to be maintained if only for the reason that it supports a free and independent way of life."

The following year, a new Crofters Commission was set up to administer the Crofter's (Scotland) Act 1955. Amendments to this Act were passed in 1961, recognising that non-agricultural use of a croft would be as valuable as the traditional ones.

The discovery of North Sea Oil and the entry of Britain into the EEC became matters of concern to the crofting community, and were closely studied by the Crofters Commission. On 10 June 1976, the Crofting Reform (Scotland) Act was passed. This, at long last, gave the crofters and cottars the right to purchase their house and ground for a nominal sum and to acquire the surrounding land at a reasonable price.

On 6 June 1997, an historic move gave Highland Crofters the chance to own, at no cost, the land they rented. Few of the crofting communities took up this offer. The new law meant that the Scottish Office could transfer 55 crofting estates it owned, together with mineral and sporting rights, to the communities. The Crofting Trust Advisory Service, set up to oversee the change, was not surprised by the slow take-up and said: "Crofting, as a system, has been in place for a long time and we are now talking about a substantial change." The Scottish Crofters' Union said: "At the moment, committees are giving it some thought, but there is no great rush, mainly because the Department of Agriculture seems a good and benevolent landlord."

The land was acquired at the turn of the century to right the wrongs of the Clearances. The Transfer of Crofting Estates (Scotland) Act 1997 means that tenants can now form a crofting trust and apply to become their own Lairds. At the time of writing, one in ten crofters, around 1,400 households, rent a total of 105,000 hectares directly from the Government.

Inchnadamph

SIXTEENTH STAGE:
Loch Ailsh to Inchnadamph (See Variant 16/17)
16 kilometres, 9.9 miles

Unlike the previous two, this stage is quite majestic; by our tastes, it is one of the best. It leaves forests and fishing, but still follows the River Oykel almost to its source at a lochan in a corrie under Ben More Assynt and eventually becomes the longest riverside journey of the whole trek (22 kilometres, from Oykel bridge to Conival).

Benmore Lodge overlooking Loch Ailsh is obviously well kept and regularly used and, being near a large forest, has an air of seclusion. On leaving the forest area, some two kilometres north of the lodge, the route enters the Ben More Assynt massif but remains low beside the Oykel. As you progress, enjoy the presence of high mountains to left and right. At the head of the glen the river tumbles steeply from its source away to the NE. Continue northwards, beside a tributary, ascending steeply in the shadow of Conival. The bealach is really a narrow gorge with the towering SW slopes of Conival rising high on your right. To your left, the slopes are also steep, but not so lofty, as they rise to Breabag Tarsuinn. In the

154

SIXTEENTH STAGE

Loch Ailsh to Inchnadamph

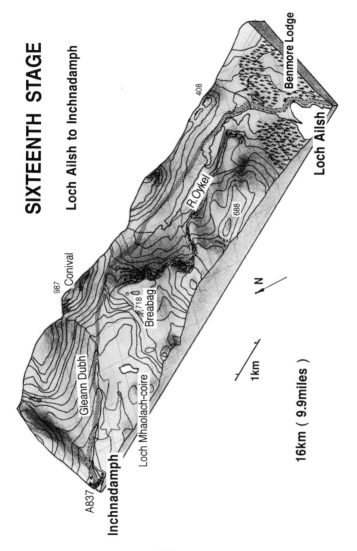

16km (9.9miles)

155

English Lake District, this would be known as 'Windy Gap'. When we were there it was a calm, sunny day, but it must be a terrible place in gale conditions.

Before entering the gorge look back southwards, down Glen Oykel. After passing through the gorge a vast panorama opens up NW over Gleann Dubh. Inchnadamph is hidden. Beyond, lies Quinag 15 kilometres away. The ascent to the gorge from Glen Oykel is rough but firm on the ground. However, lower, as you descend to Gleann Dubh, the ground is peaty and wet, hence slow. Keeping high as long as possible will minimise the amount of peat to be traversed.

A close examination of your navigation map will reveal that, on the way down Gleann Dubh, the River Traligill disappears underground and reappears 320 metres or so lower down. The fact that this is limestone country is confirmed by the nearby presence of three caves. One of them contains numerous straw stalactites. If you visit the caves, do be careful not to disturb the stalactites as they are many thousands of years old, very fragile and easily damaged.

The final descent to Inchnadamph, meaning 'stag's meadow' is easy, giving a pleasant finale to the stage. Some of the cottages, in this crofting community at the head of Loch Assynt, look as though they are built from white marble. And indeed they are, for marble is only a granular form of limestone. Four kilometres to the south, near the Allt nam Uamh, three more caves are to be found. These are geologically and archaeologically significant and have been excavated on several occasions, notably in 1917 and 1926. Many animal bones were found, and the skeletons of two humans which were dated back to 6,000 BC. Avoid entering ANY cave unless you are experienced in speleology and have the correct equipment. And remember that these caves can flood very quickly in inclement weather.

An extremely rare fish (in Scotland), the gillaroo, breeds in the excellent fishing waters hereabouts. This trout gets its name from the Gaelic *giolla ruadh*, meaning 'red lad', and has part of its stomach toughened for crushing the shells of molluscs.

There is an hotel beside the A837, which may provide meals for non-residents. There is an outdoor centre which offers accommodation, but no shop for provisions.

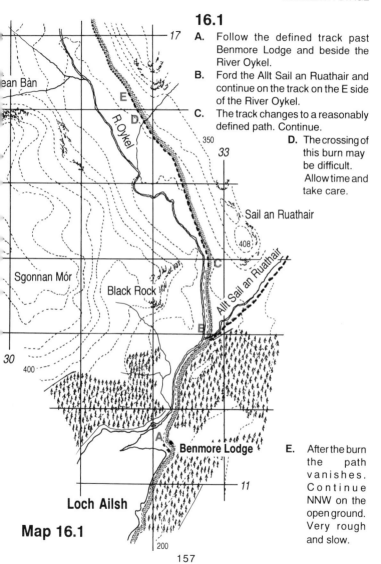

16.1

A. Follow the defined track past Benmore Lodge and beside the River Oykel.

B. Ford the Allt Sail an Ruathair and continue on the track on the E side of the River Oykel.

C. The track changes to a reasonably defined path. Continue.

D. The crossing of this burn may be difficult. Allow time and take care.

E. After the burn the path vanishes. Continue NNW on the open ground. Very rough and slow.

Map 16.1

157

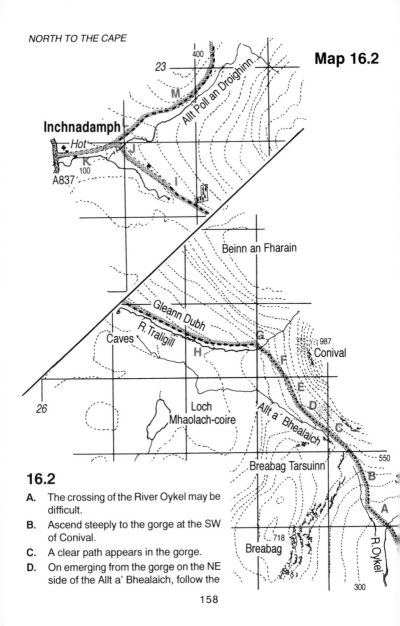

Map 16.2

16.2

A. The crossing of the River Oykel may be difficult.

B. Ascend steeply to the gorge at the SW of Conival.

C. A clear path appears in the gorge.

D. On emerging from the gorge on the NE side of the Allt a' Bhealaich, follow the path/deer trod which ascends gently, diverging from the burn. (There is a way down beside the burn, but it appears difficult. Try it if you wish.)

E. Path/trod, mostly defined. A deep gully with a rushing burn seems to block the way, so skirt around its head.

F. At the time of research, we took a lower route and encountered difficult peaty ground making the going slow. We show a higher route which may be better. Go NNW, to make for the River Traligill.

G. The river may be difficult to cross. (Lower down, it enters a gorge and will be even more difficult to cross.) Once across the river, ascend to join a defined path.

H. Follow the defined path down Gleann Dubh. (It bifurcates and rejoins, but it doesn't matter which branch you take.)

I. Join and follow the grassy track, which turns into a vehicle track.

J. The track fords the river, but there is a footbridge.

K. Descend to Inchnadamph.

L. Return to the ford (259220). Turn left just before the ford to ascend on the path.

M. Follow the defined path, which is rough in places.

Variant 16/17: **Loch Ailsh to Definitive Route near Eas a Chùal Aluinn Waterfall**
21.2 kilometres, 13.1 miles
OS Landranger 15. Loch Assynt

This route is more straightforward than the definitive one, both navigationally and on the ground. However, our opinion is that it is far less varied with fewer interesting panoramas. It goes around the eastern side of Ben More Assynt, where the slopes are far less rugged than the western side.

From Loch Ailsh, follow the definitive route past Benmore Lodge to the junction of the River Oykel with Allt Sail an Ruathair. At —

328130   keep to the SE side of the burn as the path progresses NE. We recall the path as being reasonably defined.

347173   With Loch Carn nan Conbhairean on your left, progress N.

346197   Paths join at this point. Keep ahead, just W of N.

340216	Loch na Sròine Luime is on your right.
314233	Here, OS shows the path terminating (Loch Bealach a' Mhadaidh on your left.) Cross the burn and turn NE to descend to Gorm Loch Mór. At —
315242	turn NW on the shore of the loch. At —
312247	keep NW, diverging from the shore. At —
304251	join the ascending path, continuing NW. At —
280270	join the definitive route.

TARTAN

The weaving of particoloured and multicoloured cloth cannot be claimed as modern. Nor can it be claimed as peculiar to any country or race. Weavers have been making patterned cloth since the loom was developed around 4,000 BC. Originally, the colours were white, black and brown, these shades being natural to the wool plucked from sheep and goats. But as natural dyes were developed from bark, berries, leaves and lichens, multicoloured cloth evolved.

The origin of the word tartan is not entirely clear. It may derive from the Old French *tertaine*, a variation of tiretain, which referred to a thin, coarse linen and wool mixture. It may derive from the Spanish *tirtaña*, meaning 'shiver' and referring to a fine quality cloth. Whatever its origin, tartan has been part of English language since the fifteenth century. It is a worsted cloth, woven with stripes or bands of coloured warp and weft to form a chequered pattern in which the colours alternate in 'setts' of a defined width and sequence.

When the Romans came to Britain in the first century AD, the Caledonian tribes opposing them wore striped woollen blankets draped over one shoulder. Under this blanket, precursor of the plaid, the tribesmen wore long linen shirts, sometimes with a pair of breeches.

By the eleventh century the blanket, or *feileadh mor*, Gaelic for 'large and folded', had evolved into the belted plaid. It was common throughout the Highlands. Warp length and weft widths were limited by the looms of the day to about five metres by seventy centimetres. Forerunner of the kilt, the belted plaid was made up of two lengths stitched together. There are no accurate records of exactly how the Highlanders donned the plaid. It looks as if it involved laying the plaid on the ground and pleating it until two aprons remained. The wearer then had to lie down on the plaid, gather it about his body, tie up his belt, stand up and arrange the garment to suit his own wishes. He was always careful to leave his sword arm free. It is interesting to note that in some parts of the world, notably North America, the word 'plaid' has come to mean 'tartan', the pattern. In Britain though, 'plaid', originating from the Gaelic *plaide* (pronounced 'pladjer' and meaning 'a blanket'), refers only to the garment itself.

In the 1471 accounts of John, Bishop of Glasgow and Treasurer to King James III, there occurs an item: "Ane elne and one half of blue Tartane to lyne his gowne of cloth of Gold." In 1538, a Highland dress was ordered for King James V, father of Mary, Queen of Scots, when he went on a hunting trip in the Highlands. He required "Variant cullorit velvet" for "ane schort Heland coit," and for "Heland tartane to be hose to the Kinge's grace." Bishop John Lesley wrote in 1578 that "All, both male and common people, wore mantles of one sort." He added that "The nobles preferred those of several colours". Clearly multicoloured tartan was becoming established, although the good Bishop might have been more accurate if he had pointed out that only the rich could afford coloured tartans.

Solid historical evidence that one tartan ever identified one particular clan is scarce. But by the turn of the eighteenth century, not only was coloured tartan well established but there was also inference that different tartans had indeed become associated with different regions. A native of Skye and Factor to the MacLoeds, Martin Martin, in his Description of the Western Isles of Scotland (1703) observed: "Every Isle differs from each other in their fancy of making plaids, as to the stripes in breadth and colours. This humour is as different throu the mainland of the Highlands, in so far that they who have seen these places is able, at the first view of a man's plaid, to guess the place of his residence."

The English 'philabeg', a variation of 'filibeg', derived from the Gaelic *feileadh bheag*, meaning the 'little fold', is the kilt we know today. Originally, the garment had large stitched box pleats. Our more familiar trim, tight pleats developed as a result of military influence in the nineteenth century. There is a story that an eighteenth century Glengarry ironmaster, originally from England, developed a concern for health and safety at work. He decided that the long *feileadh mor* was a safety hazard and should be shortened to the *feileadh bheag*. But this must be somewhat apocryphal; it is highly unlikely that the actions of one man alone could change the course of history in this way. It is more likely that the kilt evolved as a matter of convenience, just as women, these days, often choose a tartan skirt in preference to the full-blown kilt. However it developed, the kilt, now the Scottish National dress, is known and used worldwide.

The triubhas, or truis, close fitting breeches or trousers covering the feet, rather like modern tights, were worn, sometimes with the belted plaid, on horseback. Certain Scottish regiments still wear trews, which being footless are not, strictly speaking, truis.

The battle of Culloden on 16 April 1746 led to the downfall of Bonnie Prince Charlie, to the dismantling of the feudal clan system and to a ban on tartan dress (except for those in the army). In the '45 Rising, many Jacobite supporters had slept in the long plaid, refusing to use tents. They would sometimes soak the plaid in water, wring it out, and envelop their bodies in the damp material so that they could sleep in a kind of steamy heat. So attached were they to their native form of dress, that they were incensed to learn:

"… From the first day of August 1747, no man or boy within that part of Great Britain called Scotland, other then such as shall be employed as officers and soldiers in His Majesty's forces, shall, on any pretence whatsoever wear, or put on the clothes commonly called Highland clothes, (that is to say the plaid, philabeg or little kilt, trowse, shoulder belts, or any part whatsoever of what peculiarly belongs to the Highland garb …" It went on to say that if this was not strictly adhered to, those convicted: "… shall suffer imprisonment without bail, during the space of six months, and no longer: and being convicted for a second offence … shall be liable to be transported to any of His Majesty's plantations for the space of seven years."

The rigorously enforced ban was met with deep rooted, widespread resentment. But it was not until 1782 that one of the founders of the Highland Society of London, the Marquis of Graham, appealed to Parliament to have the ban repealed. He was successful and the rebirth of tartan was met with exultation. The resulting announcement proclaimed: "Listen men! This is bringing before all the sons of the Gael, that the King and Parliament of Britain have for ever abolished the Act against Highland dress; which came down to the clans from the beginning of the world to the year 1746. You are no longer bound down to the unmanly dress of the Lowlander. This is declaring to every man young and old, single and gentle, that they may after this put on and wear the truis, the little kilt, the coat and the striped hose, as also the belted plaid without fear of the law of the realm or the spite of the enemies."

Tartan achieved wide popularity in the early nineteenth century, not least through the prolific writings of the Scottish novelist and poet Sir Walter Scott. It was he who promoted the visit to Edinburgh of King George IV in 1822, the first monarch to visit Scotland since Charles II in 1650. The occasion was a time for great celebration. Heads of families, and many others, wore tartan; any tartan. The festivities firmly established tartan as very much a part of Scottish culture.

Nineteenth century mills brought out catalogues of their tartan patterns, including some which were attributed to clan or family names at the whim of the mill owner. Today, there are over 2,000 various tartans and much effort has been put into researching their authenticity: the Scottish Tartan Society lists all known tartans and registers new ones; the Scottish Lyon King at Arms and the Standing Council of Scottish Chiefs are supposed to approve all new tartans. There is no record, however, of anyone being dispatched to the dungeons of Edinburgh Castle for bypassing these authorities.

Seeing and hearing a pipe major and his pipers in full Highland uniform is a romantic, stirring sight thousands flock to see. The kilt and plaid are worn not only at ceremonial occasions, but at weddings, festivals, ceilidhs and many other social events. Over the years many accoutrements have been devised to enhance the wearing of the kilt:

- A Balmoral hat (so called because of its association with the royal residence), rather like a blue beret, may be worn.
- Shirt and tie are as the wearer wishes, but tweed jackets (green and brown) are normal.
- Plain leather belts, with polished brass buckles, have been joined by belts and buckles in a wide variety of designs and materials.
- The sporran (Gaelic for 'purse'), was once made from goat or deer skin and used to be worn on the hip. Now, other modern materials are used and the sporran is worn at the front, with stud fasteners instead of laces.
- The kilt pin was introduced by Queen Victoria, who wished her

163

soldiers to be paragons of propriety.

- Knitted stockings are a relatively recent addition. They used to be made from the same fibres as the kilt.

- The boy scout-like 'tabs' on the stockings are relics of ribbon garters from times past.

- The knife tucked into the stocking top is the *sgian dubh*, or 'black knife', so called because unpolished metal was used in its manufacture. Nowadays symbolic, it was originally an implement for skinning animals or eating with.

- Shoes worn with Highland dress are a matter of personal preference. Black shoes are conventional for evening wear and the English brogue is from the Gaelic *brog*, meaning 'shoe'. The holes punched in the leather of today's brogues are symbolic of the holes made in the Highlanders' deerskin footwear. They were originally made to let out water which inevitably collected when crossing rivers or in the wet.

Victorian music hall comedians used to ask "Well do they, or don't they"? The answer is "Yes and no". Underwear beneath the kilt is a relatively recent addition. The men of several Scottish regiments still wear nothing under the kilt, except when on sentry duty or dancing. Other men wear their own preferred underwear. Or do they?

Whether you be a Campbell or a Cameron, a Forbes or a Fraser, a Gordon or a Grant, a McCraner or even a Brook, wear your tartan with pride. it has rich historic associations.

Kylesku

SEVENTEENTH STAGE:
Inchnadamph to Kylesku (See Variant 16/17)
18.2 kilometres, 11.3 miles

If you have ever travelled between Inchnadamph and Kylesku on the A837 and A894 and looked eastwards from time to time, you may remember the vast uninterrupted SW face of the Glas Bheinn massif. This uniform wall belies the rugged landscape beyond, through which our trek passes. The first half of this stage covers the last of the relatively high, craggy country, giving splendid vistas east and north. The region to the west, including Quinag, is hidden behind Glas Bheinn until the second half of the stage, when Quinag becomes the dominant feature.

The climb out of Inchnadamph is quite steep, rising from 50 metres to over 400 metres in less than three kilometres. The path is defined albeit rough.

The route then becomes tortuous, convoluted, dotted with lochans and must, in theory, be magical; when we were there we were navigating on compass through cloud and rain.

165

SEVENTEENTH STAGE

Inchnadamph to Kylesku

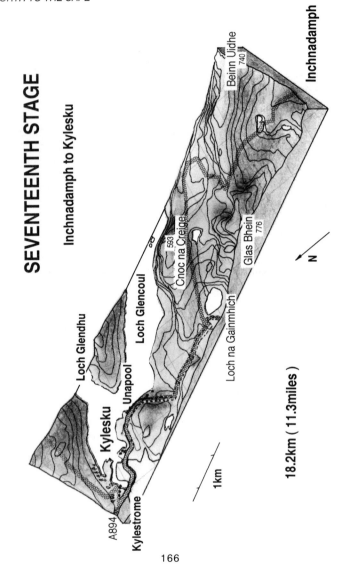

Inchnadamph

Beinn Uidhe
740

Glas Bhein
776

Loch na Gainmhich

Chnoc na Creige
593

Loch Glencoul

Loch Glendhu

Unapool

Kylesku

Kylestrome

A894

N

1km

18.2km (11.3miles)

A return journey of about 1.5 kilometres will afford you a view of the highest waterfall in the British Isles (the highest single leap is in Gaping Gill in Yorkshire). It is well worth the time and effort. The Eas a Chùal Aluinn, pronounced 'Ess Cool Allin', is four times the height of the Niagara. The 198 metre falls descend a sheer cliff of the Leiter Dhubh in two leaps into the dark glen which heads Loch Beag, a continuation of Loch Glencoul.

The second half of this stage is a road walk from Loch na Gainmhich to Kylesku. We studied long and hard to find a cross-country way. The only one that was possible, and which used substantially OS paths, was around the shores of Lochs Glencoul and Glendhu but this would have made the stage uncomfortably long. Also, Kylesku, with its limited facilities, would not have been a natural stopping place. Kylesku is no longer on the main thoroughfare, but is quaint and interesting. There is an hotel and B & B accommodation, but no shop.

In 1983, when we first did this trek, the bridge across the kyle was under construction and the ferry was still operational giving, for us, a more romantic touch to the journey than does the plod across the bridge. The Kylesku Bridge now links Kylesku with Kylestrome, replacing the ferry and spanning the junctions of Lochs Glendhu and Glencoul with Loch a' Chàirn Bhàin on the A894. It was opened by the Queen in 1984.

17.1 (see map p168)

A.   Follow the defined path, which is rough in places.

B.   Keep left (NNW) where the path bifurcates.

C.   The path becomes unclear on the peat but keep N, then descend to the W end of Loch Fleodach Coire.

D.   A broken bridge spans the river, but it can be used with care. (The wooden slats may be slippery.) Ascend N from the loch.

E.   Turn NW, ascending all the way. The path is unclear, but the cairns help.

F.   On reaching the bealach, make sure you find the defined path for the descent. Cairns help.

G.   The first part of the descent is very steep and rough, but well defined.

H.   The path is not well defined, lower down, where it crosses peat and grass. Your general direction should be ENE.

I.   Turn N to round a rocky spur and reach a pair of lochans at:

J.   Pass between them, then turn left (N) on the unclear path. Do NOT proceed

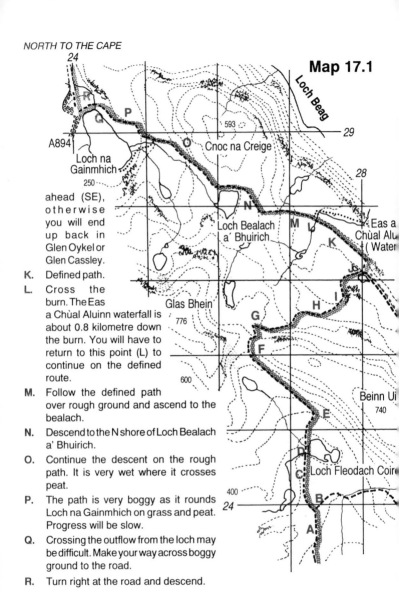

Map 17.1

ahead (SE), otherwise you will end up back in Glen Oykel or Glen Cassley.

K. Defined path.

L. Cross the burn. The Eas a Chùal Aluinn waterfall is about 0.8 kilometre down the burn. You will have to return to this point (L) to continue on the defined route.

M. Follow the defined path over rough ground and ascend to the bealach.

N. Descend to the N shore of Loch Bealach a' Bhuirich.

O. Continue the descent on the rough path. It is very wet where it crosses peat.

P. The path is very boggy as it rounds Loch na Gainmhich on grass and peat. Progress will be slow.

Q. Crossing the outflow from the loch may be difficult. Make your way across boggy ground to the road.

R. Turn right at the road and descend.

Map 17.2

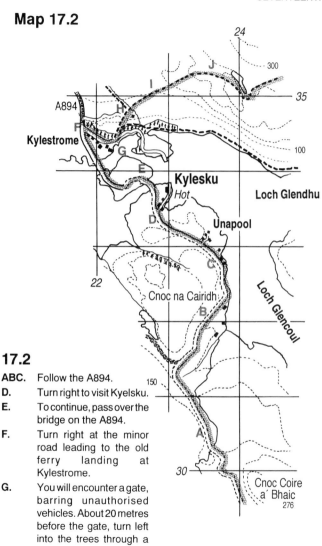

17.2

ABC. Follow the A894.

D. Turn right to visit Kyelsku.

E. To continue, pass over the bridge on the A894.

F. Turn right at the minor road leading to the old ferry landing at Kylestrome.

G. You will encounter a gate, barring unauthorised vehicles. About 20 metres before the gate, turn left into the trees through a gap in the fence. Ascend on the track to the metalled lane at:

H.   Cross the lane and ascend on the track/path.

I.   You will find a number of paths leading off the main route. Keep to the one which proceeds ENE and appears to be the ancient and original one.

J.   The track/path is well defined.

Recipe for Sutherland

Take a mass of northern land
With heads and capes and lochs and isles
Where waters sourced from sea and spring
Dance to the tune of the Beaufort Scale
Twirling about the compass

Blend cubes of rock with rising ground
Form into mounts that reach for the heels
Of the jostling clouds as they tumble and bloom
Like ceilings of steam in a kitchen
Seeking a means of escape

Stir till the sun in moments blue
Souses and drenches and moistens the light
In wavelets and plumes brought forth by the wind
Buffeting your bones with its random affronts
Flap-flapping your view with your sleeve

Steep in a marinadeof tides
From Malin from Faeroes and Iceland
Season with heather and drizzle with moss
Bake in the warmest of Greenwich meantimes
Brushing edges with birch and goat willow

MUNRO, CORBETT AND DONALD

No, not a firm of dentists, doctors or solicitors, but three men who are remembered for their contributions to the delightful pastimes of walking and climbing.

Sir Hugh Thomas Munro (1861-1919) was born in London the eldest son of Campbell Munro of Lindertis, also a 'Sir'. Inheriting the family estate near Kirriemuir, H T Munro was an enthusiastic traveller and became a founder member of the Scottish Mountaineering Club (SMC) in 1889. He compiled the first authoritative list of what have become known as 'Munros', and he published this list as his *Table of Heights Over Three Thousand Feet* in the first issue of the SMC Journal in 1891. To be included in the list, a summit must be 3,000 feet (914 metres) or more in height and be separated from other summits by a drop of 500 feet (153 metres) or more, by a considerable distance or by a natural obstacle. Munro did not have any clear definitions of what a 'considerable distance' or a 'natural obstacle' is.

The magical figure of 3,000 feet can never really be replaced by its metric equivalent of 914.4 metres. Munro tables and maps list heights in both metres and feet and the number of Munros has changed over the years, the first table of 238 Scottish summits being revised several times in pace with new methods of measuring heights. By 1921 there were 276 Munros, 279 in 1953 and 276 in 1981 when more changes took place. In 1990, the Ordnance Survey reassessed the height of a peak, previously thought to be under 3,000 feet, and the number reached 277.

As well as Munros the SMC lists 'tops'. Each top must be 3,000 feet or more in height and be quite distinct from other summits or tops. Again, Munro did not define 'quite distinct from'. The Club has very recently reclassified one summit and eight tops, making the present totals 284 summits and 233 tops.

There are eight summits over four thousand feet (1219 metres) in Scotland, four in Lochaber and four in the Cairngorms. They are accompanied by 13 tops.

Several hundred Munro baggers have climbed every Munro, and mountaineer Hamish Brown was the first person to bag them all in a single trip. As one might expect, record breakers have been attracted by the obvious challenge of climbing all the Munros and, incidentally, many tops in the shortest possible time. The current record was set by Hugh

Symonds, who took a mere 66 days and 22 hours to travel between Ben Hope and Ben Lomond from 19 April to 25 June 1990. He covered 2,211 kilometres and climbed a total of 128,600 metres. He rowed to Skye, sailed to Mull and ran between the summits.

The record for the eight 4,000 foot summits, traversing 136 kilometres from Glen Nevis to Glen More, was set by Martin Stone on 4 July 1987 and stands at 21 hours 39 minutes. The Scottish 24 hour record is 28 Munros from Clunie Inn, with 10,668 metres of ascents, set by Jon Broxap on 30/31 July 1988.

Hugh Munro, who was honoured by being elected President of the SMC between 1894 and 1897, attempted to climb all 'his' summits, dressed in a kilt and a Balmoral cap. Tragically, he died of pneumonia in France before he could tackle the last two. One was the Inaccessible Peak on Skye, the only one to require ropes for its ascent. The other was Carn Clioch - mhulinn in the Cairngorms, which he had been saving until last.

The Scottish Mountaineering Club's 'Munro's Tables of the 3,000ft Mountains' also includes 'And Other Tables of Lesser Heights'. Following in Munro's footsteps, J. Rooke Corbett compiled his Corbett's Tables. This is a list of Scottish Mountains 2,500 feet (762 metres) and under 3,000 feet in height, with re-ascents of 500 feet (152 metres) on all sides. This list is not strictly comparable with those compiled by Munro or Donald, as it does not profess to include all the relevent summits and tops which, were it to do so on a Munro or Donald basis, would give a much larger total.

Percy Donald's Tables list 'All Hills in the Scottish Lowlands 2,000 feet (610 metres) in Height and Above. Donald's Tables are accompanied by definitions in which he describes 'tops' as 'All elevations with a drop of more than 100 feet (30.48 metres) on all sides and elevations of sufficient topographical merit with a drop of between 100 feet and 50 feet (15.25 metres) on all sides'. The grouping of tops into 'hills', except where inapplicable on topographical grounds, is on a basis that tops are not more than 17 units from the main top of the hill to which they belong. A 'unit' is either $1/12$ mile (0.13 kilometre) measured along the connecting ridge, or one 50 foot contour between the lower top and its connecting col.

On your trip to and through the Western Highlands you will see many mountains. Enjoy them all, whether they be Munros, Corbetts or Donalds.

Eas a Chùal Aluinn

EIGHTEENTH STAGE:
Kylesku to Achfary
13.5 kilometres, 8.4 miles

From Kylesku, you will require provisions for three days.

This is another short stage, which will be welcome after the previous one. Also, navigation is straightforward and the ground presents no problems; the route is defined all the way. All this may project a rather banal image, but this is far from the case. Every step of the way presents stupendous panoramas; including the road walk over the bridge with its views over the sea lochs. South-west, towards the sea, and over Loch a' Chàirn Bhàin, the landmass is dominated by Quinag (809 metres). It takes its name from the Gaelic *Cuinneg* meaning 'milk stoup', which it is said to resemble. On a fine day, the ascent from the road is spellbinding. The vast bulk of Quinag with its seven tops still rules, and the lochs and

173

EIGHTEENTH STAGE

Kylesku to Achfary

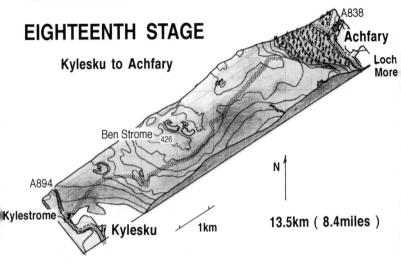

13.5km (8.4miles)

Kylesku vie for your attention down below.

Higher still, the panorama expands to include Loch Glencoul, south and Loch Glendhu, east. From this point we were able to make out a long white trail in the far distance, which we concluded to be Eas a Chùal Aluinn, about eight kilometres away. Later, as the route ascends more gently in a north-easterly direction, pause to look south-east at the vast amphitheatre cradling Loch an Leathiad Bhuain.

The pleasant, easy finale to the stage along the A838 runs beside Loch More for a short distance, with Achfary Forest keeping you company all the way on the left. Achfary seems to be an estate community and the only public facility is a rare sight, a telephone box painted black and white.

174

18.1

ABC. Follow the well-defined path, boggy on higher level ground. Don't count on sheltering in the shieling, it is a ruin.

D. The descent is fairly steep and enters the forest at:

E. Continue on the track through the forest.

F. Pass through the gate ahead and onto the well-made estate track. Follow this to the cottages and to the road (A838).

G. Turn left and follow the road to Achfary.

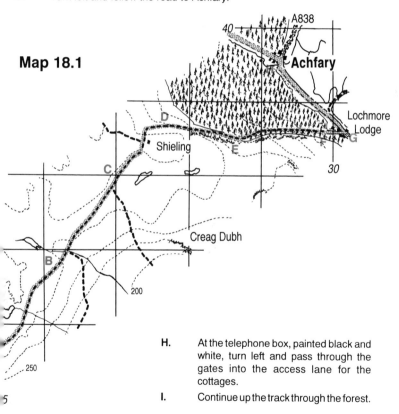

Map 18.1

H. At the telephone box, painted black and white, turn left and pass through the gates into the access lane for the cottages.

I. Continue up the track through the forest.

NAISMITH AND TRANTER

Having walked together for many years, we authors have a precise understanding of each other's walking abilities over all sorts of terrain. This enables us, fairly accurately, to forecast the time it will take us to cover a certain distance, taking into account the many variables which inevitably arise. If you have not enjoyed the privilege of a long-time walking partner, or are still developing your walking skills, you may care to utilise Naismith's Rule to work out the time it will take you to cover a route:

Allow one hour for every five kilometres (three miles) measured on the map, plus an additional half-hour for every 300 metres (1,000 feet) climbed.

The distance climbed is the sum total of all the ascents.

The use of this Rule assumes that a walker is of average fitness. It does not take account of inclement weather, conditions underfoot, the weight of the rucksack or pauses for navigation.

So, how does one adapt Naismith's Rule (W. Naismith was a Scottish climber) to take account of these variables? Philip Tranter (another Scottish climber?) formulated a variation to the Rule as follows:

| Fitness | Time Taken in Minutes According to Naismith's Rule | | | | | | | | | |
Level	60	120	180	240	300	360	420	480	540	600
15	30	60	90	120	165	210	270	330	405	465
20	40	75	135	195	270	330	390	465	525	600
25	50	90	180	255	330	420	510	600	690	795
30	60	120	210	300	405	510	630	750	870	
35	70	145	230	320	425	540	660	MORE		
40	80	165	255	345	450	570	690	THAN CAN BE		
45	90	180	270	365	480			COMFORTABLY		
50	100	195	285	390	510			WALKED		

To use the Variations you must first calculate your fitness level, or that of the weakest member where a group is involved. Find out the time taken to climb 300 metres (1,000 feet) in 800 metres (half-a-mile), from a fresh start, with no rests and at a normal pace. If it takes 35 minutes, for example, then the fitness level is 35. Having established the first step, the

variation can be applied. For example, using Naismith's Rule:
A walk of 10 kilometres with a total height gain of 700 metres will take three hours and twelve minutes.
Applying Tranter's Variation to the fitness level of 35 gives an estimated time of 248 minutes; say four-and-a-quarter hours.

We have studied Tranter's table and think that there are inconsistencies, but the figures are quoted unchanged from the original. If you decide to use Naismith's Rule and Tranter's Variations frequently, you can produce your own graphs to reach an easy interpolation of intermediate values.

The Variations may also be used to account for other conditions. For instance:
Drop one fitness level for every 13 kilograms weight of rucksack.
Drop one fitness level for strong winds or poor visibility.
Drop one fitness level for waterlogged or slippery conditions.
Drop up to four fitness levels for snow.

Also, it is important to allow additional time for meal stops, navigation stops and the fact that a party of walkers will always go slower than an individual or a couple.

When walking in the mountains, and especially in the Western Highlands of Scotland, it is of prime importance that you estimate your travel times accurately. Failure to do so could have dire consequences.

We think that Naismith's Rule is too simple and that Tranter's Variations are too complicated. When walking in the Highlands and the mountainous areas of England and Wales, our rule of thumb is:
Allow three kilometres per hour, plus a half-hour for every six kilometres as measured on the map
A walk of 10 kilometres will take $10/3 + .75 \approx 4$ hours.
A walk of 15 kilometres will take $15/3 + 1.5 \approx 6.5$ hours.

Of necessity, research is very slow, as one has to pause many times for navigational purposes. Indeed, we have on some occasions had to retrace our steps in order to get the route correct. If we are walking only for pleasure, minor navigational errors are of no consequence. Unless you are a very fit and robust walker, we suggest that you use 'Brook and Hinchliffe's Rule' (about 2.3 kilometres/hour), especially if you are carrying a heavy rucksack and are in unfamiliar country. Always overestimate the time. It is better to arrive early than late or not at all.

Achfary

NINETEENTH STAGE:
Achfary to Rhiconich (See Variant 19)
20 kilometres, 12.4 miles

A fairly long stage; just over 200 metres at the highest point, but below 100 metres for most of the way. The first part, between Achfary and Lochstack Lodge, skirts round Ben Stack on quite well-defined paths. The next five kilometres or so, after the lodge, is also on a good path. However, the following four kilometres is demanding and wet with no path except, perhaps, for an angler's 'trod' alongside Loch a' Garbh-bhaid Mór. The fording of Garbh Allt can be difficult, so expect to be delayed and to get wet feet. The final few kilometres into Rhiconich follow a well-defined path.

The best view of Ben Stack will be seen by looking back from the path beyond Lochstack Lodge. Ahead from this point, Arkle rises steeply some two kilometres away. Another view of Arkle will be possible from the head of Loch a' Garbh-bhaid Mór, again looking backwards.

Apart from these two mountains, the terrain is low level for many kilometres around. It is dotted with literally hundreds of lochans, making very difficult walking away from the paths.

Rhiconich has an hotel, which provides meals for non-residents, but there are no facilities for provisions.

NINETEENTH STAGE
Part A   Achfary to Lochstack Lodge

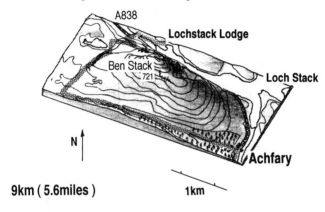

9km (5.6miles)

Part B   Lochstack Lodge to Rhiconich

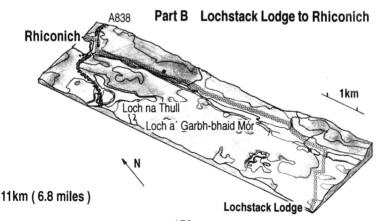

11km (6.8 miles)

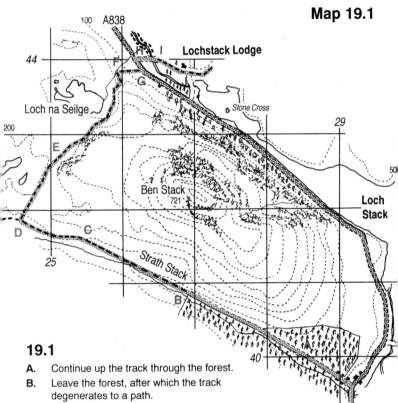

Map 19.1

19.1

A. Continue up the track through the forest.

B. Leave the forest, after which the track degenerates to a path.

C. Higher up, the path becomes ill defined. Very wet and rough.

D. Turn right on reaching the defined path.

E. Continue on the well-defined path.

F. The descent is steep, but easy.

G. At the road, turn left for about 200 metres then:

H. Turn right into the track leading to the footbridge across the river.

I. After crossing the bridge, turn right on the path.

J. Keep Lochstack Lodge on your left until you join its driveway. Walk along the drive for a few metres, then ahead onto a well-defined path.

Note! If you are in a hurry and don't mind a route march, you can leave Achfary on the A838 and walk to the driveway of Lochstack Lodge. Turn into it and over the bridge to join the definitive route.

19.2

ABC. Follow the well-defined path.

D. After crossing the Alltan Riabhach, leave the path to proceed NW across very rough ground. No path, rocky and wet.

E. At the head of Loch a' Garbh-bhaid Mór, keep to its E bank. A path of sorts, but very rough and very wet.

F. Continue on the E bank.

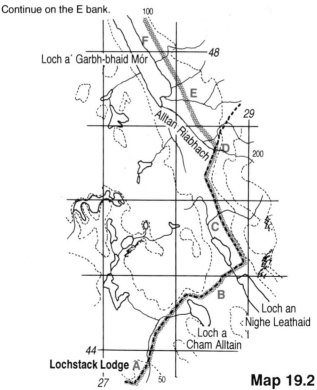

Map 19.2

19.3

A.   Keep to the E of the burn to the head of Loch a' Gharb-bhaid Beag, and continue on the rough path. Very wet in places.

B.   Ford the Garbh Allt.

C.   Join the path and follow it to Rhiconich and the A838.

D.   Turn right at the A838, then bear left onto the B801.

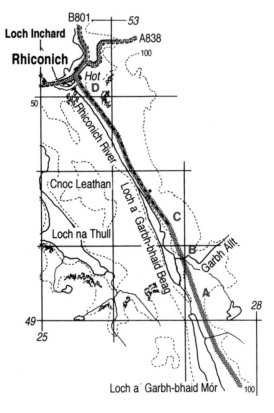

Map 19.3

Variant 19: **Achfary to Definitive Route under Arkle**
7.3 kilometres, 4.5 miles
OS Landranger 9. Cape Wrath

This is a shorter and low level route, mainly beside Loch Stack. About half of the way is on a track (estate road), followed by pathless open country where the going is rough.

Leave Achfary on the A838 towards Laxford Bridge. After about one kilometre, at —

297402	turn right, leaving the road to enter the track and cross the bridge over the river. Continue on the track to the next river at —
309422	Cross the river via the bridge, after which there are diverging paths. Turn NNW, leaving the paths and make for the shore of Loch Stack (no path). Follow the shore to the NW end of the Loch. At —
291436	continue, leaving the loch behind and ascending to follow the burn. At —
286443	descend, following another burn. At —
287450	join the definitive route.

WHISKY

In the last 40 years or so, we have visited Scotland many times. Each trip included a visit to, and usually a stay in, the Western Highlands. Being well aware of the vagaries of the Scottish weather, we always assume that it will rain every day. If any day is fine, then that is a bonus. Intensity of rain in Scotland is in the eye of the beholder. What we Sassenachs call drizzle, the Scots call haar. What we call steady rain, they call drizzle. What we call a downpour, they find 'a wee bit damp'. It's perhaps as well that it does rain a lot in Scotland, otherwise we would not enjoy the magnificent mountains with lochans, lochs, rivers and waterfalls. Furthermore, we would not be able to enjoy Scotland's great gift to the world: whisky. For it is the abundance of clean, fresh water, from many different sources, that has made Scotch Whisky in its many varieties.

Dictionaries provide a rather objective definition of whisky: a distilled spirit made from cereals. As a word, whisky is derived from the late-sixteenth century *usquebaugh*, itself derived from the Gaelic *uisge-beatha* meaning 'water of life'; a much more romantic definition. The first record of whisky distilling in Scotland is dated 1494, although in those days the product would have been flavoured with sugar, saffron, nutmeg and other spices. It is thought, however, that distilling was carried out in Scotland at least three centuries before this. In Ireland the word 'whiskey' is derived from the same Gaelic root, and this same word describes similar products distilled in America. The use of the word 'Scotch' as an alternative to Scots or Scottish should be avoided, especially in Scotland, as it may be regarded as somewhat offensive. 'Scotch' is acceptable to describe whisky, but it would betray the fact that you were a stranger to these matters. Ask for whisky, and all will be well.

There are three principal groups of whisky: malt, grain and a blend of these two. Production processes are similar in that they involve distillation, but there the similarity ends. They are all very different products.

The term 'single malt' refers to whisky produced by a single distillery, sold unblended and unadulterated after maturation. There are over 100 malt whisky distillers in the Highlands and Islands of Scotland but, alas, there are not over 100 malts for sale, as some of these distilleries devote their entire output to blending processes.

A small proportion of single malts is combined with a selection of other single malts to produce vatted malts. These are considered acceptable by some buffs, but most agree that they are not up to the same standard as a single malt. When sampling a single malt, you can be certain what you are drinking. That is not the case with vatted malts, as the labels rarely describe the origin or number of the constituent malts.

Grain whisky is a different product entirely. It is often described as an insipid colourless liquid, suitable only for blending. It is difficult to find, but it does have its devotees. Grain whisky production, with one exception, is confined to Southern Scotland. Compared with malt whisky the output of grain is enormous, but there are only about fifteen grain distilleries due to the nature of the production process.

By contrast, blended whisky is easy to find. You can buy it almost worldwide. It has been around much longer and is perhaps even more widely known than the ubiquitous Coca-Cola. Stores, markets, supermarkets, hypermarkets all display bewildering arrays of the many whisky varieties. Licensed premises offer a wide choice of several blends, and they are used, with other spirits and mixers, as a basis for cocktails everywhere. As the name suggests, blended whisky is a combination of grain whisky (around 50 per cent) and (sometimes many) malt whiskies. One blending house boasts a library of over 600 different malts. The art of the blender is to produce a whisky that looks nice, tastes nice and is suitable for mass consumption. The blender, with his sensitive nose, is all-important in achieving that fine balance between 'drinkable' and 'good' blends. Price, of course, is an overall consideration.

So, how is whisky made? It is beyond the scope of this feature to give step-by-step details of the many processes, but a brief description may be of interest.

Three simple ingredients are required to produce malt whisky: barley (mostly grown in Scotland), peat, and soft water. The water, usually from a local well or burn, is crucial in giving the whisky its characteristic flavour. The barley is first dried and then steeped in water for two or three days. The water is drained off and the soggy barley tipped onto the malting floor. Germination begins; this process being helped by turning and spreading the barley. Most distilleries nowadays use mechanical equipment to execute this back-breaking work. Next, the 'green malt' is dried in a peat-fired kiln. The peaty smoke, percolating through the malt, gives flavour to the final product, although most distilleries incorporate more efficient fuels with the peat for this stage. Kiln chimneys are characteristically pagoda-shaped, standing out above the otherwise architecturally insignificant wharehouse-like buildings of the distilleries. Dedicated malting firms are frequently used to carry out this time-consuming process, to specifications provided by their distiller clients.

The dried malt is then milled and the resulting grist is put into mash tuns. A large distillery will stir ten tonnes of malted barley into 50,000 litres of warm water. The resultant hot wort is fermented by adding a precise amount of yeast. At this stage, the frothy, bubbling liquid becomes a low strength alcohol, called wash. The wash is fed into the giant, gleaming, copper stills where double, sometimes triple, distillation takes place. This final stage yields a colourless, fiery, raw spirit (70% alcohol) which has taken about three weeks to produce. It is reduced with distilled water to about 40% by volume. A long period of 'hibernation' follows before the product can be offered for sale.

Whereas malt whisky has a discrete process, with each distillation being separate from the next, the production of grain whisky is a continuous process. Much of the groundwork for both is similar. The bulk of the cereal used for making grain whisky is maize, mixed with a small quantity of barley. The cereals are malted, mashed and then distilled. The continuous stills produce vast quantities of grain spirits, usually considered to have much less character than malt.

After distillation, the spirit must, by UK law, be matured for at least three years before being offered for consumption. Whilst the law applies to all whiskies, it is the malt which benefits more from this enforced dormancy. The casks, traditionally old sherry casks, colour the whisky naturally. When demand exceeded supply, new, wine-treated, oak casks were made. Nowadays, a brown syrupy substance called pajorete is used to soak the casks. At the time of writing, newspapers were reporting that Scottish scientists had discovered a way to make whisky mature more quickly. This involves pressing a mixture of table salt into the barrel staves and heating them under an electric burner thus, allegedly, producing barrels that will mature the whisky more quickly. Unlike malt, a grain whisky will gain little from extended maturation. A five-year-old malt will be far superior to one which has been matured for the statutory minimum of three years. A ten-year-old malt will be one of considerable merit. Add five years and the whisky will have a stature to compare with the finest Cognacs. There is much doubt as to whether malt whisky improves when matured more than fifteen years. One thing is sure: unlike some wines, malt whisky will not improve, or deteriorate, in the bottle.

The label on the bottle is all important, as this gives, or should give, you the information you will need when selecting a bottle from the host of available varieties. Many labels contain information which is virtually meaningless. Words such as ancient, cream, extra, finest, matured, old, reserve, special and so on mean little, as they are not defined within the trade. As well as the name of the whisky, you should expect to find the words 'Scotch Whisky' on the label. 'Product of Scotland' must be there, as must be 'Distilled Blended and Bottled in Scotland'. Finally, the amount of whisky, usually 75 centilitres (cl), as well as the alcoholic strength, usually 40% Vol, must be present. The last two are particularly important, as retailers have been known to supply blends in smaller bottles and/or with lower strengths to make the price more attractive. Incidentally, most of the price of a bottle of whisky goes to the Exchequer. Spirits in general and whisky in particular have been a profitable source of tax, since the imposition of excise duty in 1644 led to two centuries of determined and profitable smuggling. Things calmed down following a more reasonable act of Parliament in 1823.

Which bottle should you select? It all depends! If you intend to serve whisky with mixers, such as American Ginger Ale, almost any blend will do. Most supermarkets have their own label blends, often sold in one litre and one-and-a-half litre bottles at promotional prices. These blends can be very good. However if you want the real thing, identified by the words 'single malt' and sold at roughly twice the price, then your choice is very different. Perhaps you should try the less peaty ones such as Glenfiddich, Glen Grant or a Glenmorangie (rhymes with 'orangey'). The mediums such as Blair Athol or Balvenie may be more to your liking than the heavies such as Laphroig or Talisker. If you are buying duty free, you may find strengths increased, and these may also be available from specialist outlets. Plain water, preferably soft, should be added to your dram. This helps to release the flavours. Ice should never be added. You could, of course, really splash out and try to find a 40-year-old Bowmore. You will have to pay at least £4,000 for a bottle of this limited edition of only 306 bottles of the Islay distillery's 1955 production.

Whatever your choice, whisky can be enjoyed at any time of day. It is particularly delightful as a pre- or post-prandial drink. If you've never sampled the 'water of life' your trip in the Highlands will provide you with every opportunity to do so. It's a must with a dish of haggis.

Sandwood Bay

TWENTIETH STAGE:
Rhiconich to Blairmore
12 kilometres, 7.4 miles

When you leave Kinlochbervie, you will require provisions for three days.

When designing a trekking route, many alternatives present themselves and the factors in the selection include practicalities and personal preference. Mostly, there is little difficulty in choosing. However, in this case we had a dilemma: should we take the straightforward road walk from Rhiconich through Kinlochbervie to Blairmore, or pioneer a cross-country route from the A838 Durness road to Sandwood Bay? We finally chose the former, because we felt the variety of scenery, the lochside walk, the communities, the facilities and the interest at the fishing village of Kinlochbervie outweighed the disadvantage of the road walk. We judged the latter to be an unspectacular plod across difficult and probably wet country, with no facilities. However, our choice does not have to be yours. If you abhor road walking, do find a cross-country route.

The B801 (there aren't many B roads in this part of Scotland) from Rhiconich to Kinlochbervie is newly widened and easy, albeit twisting. Presumably it has been modernised to give good vehicular access to the fishing harbour from the modernised A838 and the A895. When we first visited this area in the 1960s, all the roads were single track with passing places which made what is now a half-hour journey twice as long.

Being a short stage we do recommend one or two diversions to explore the small communities, in particular a browse around the harbour at Kinlochbervie. You will find it a surprisingly busy place, as it is the most important fishing village in the North-west Highlands.

There is a shop, named The London Stores, on the B801 just before the village. It once claimed to be the furthest shop on the west coast of mainland Britain from the city which bears its name. However, there is another shop and a bakery on the new, small industrial estate in Kinlochbervie, which now lay claim to the distinction of being the last shops in the west. There are two hotels in the village, and one or two B & Bs off route near Blairmore; we went to look at those at Sheigra and Oldshore Beg.

It is recorded in the thirteenth century Manuscript of the Haken Saga that, in 1263, King Haken of Norway sailed south from the Orkneys to help

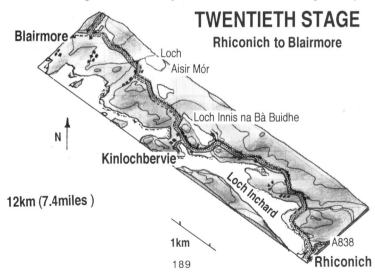

TWENTIETH STAGE

Rhiconich to Blairmore

Blairmore

Loch Aisir Mór

Loch Innis na Bà Buidhe

N

Kinlochbervie

Loch Inchard

12km (7.4miles)

1km

A838

Rhiconich

right the wrongs inflicted on the inhabitants of Skye. Having rounded the Cape, his 100 ships anchored near the northern entrance to Loch Inchard. He named this anchorage Asleifarvie. This has been badly corrupted to give the name Oldshore Beg.

Map 20.1

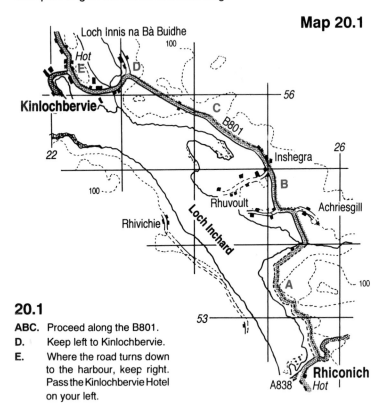

20.1

ABC. Proceed along the B801.

D. Keep left to Kinlochbervie.

E. Where the road turns down to the harbour, keep right. Pass the Kinlochbervie Hotel on your left.

20.2

ABC. Continue on the minor road.

D. Opposite the car park, turn right into the track and through the gate.

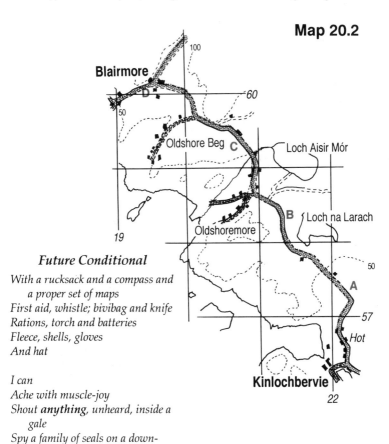

Map 20.2

Future Conditional

With a rucksack and a compass and
   a proper set of maps
First aid, whistle; bivibag and knife
Rations, torch and batteries
Fleece, shells, gloves
And hat

I can
Ache with muscle-joy
Shout **anything**, unheard, inside a
   gale
Spy a family of seals on a down-
   there sandbank
Pump my lungs with happiness
   and clean, clean air

Nearly There

TWENTY-FIRST STAGE:
Blairmore to Cape Wrath
19 kilometres, 11.8 miles

The Final Stage!

The route from the car park at Blairmore to Sandwood Bay presents no real difficulty, beyond a wet, boggy path in places. Scenery-wise it is unremarkable, crossing featureless moorland for many a long mile. Just after leaving Blairmore look backwards: the scenery is much more interesting. The ultimate reward for this trudge is the charm and isolation of Sandwood Bay. Were it not six kilometres from a motor road, it would be ideal for young families. When we were first at Blairmore, there was neither car park nor a

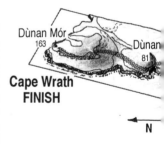

19km (11.8miles)

gate and it was possible to get a vehicle well down the track. From a walker's point of view, it is as well that there is now no vehicular access. You may find it strategically advantageous to camp at the Bay, perhaps at the NE corner of Sandwood Loch, which is a fresh-water loch. It is a popular place, so do remember the countryside code.

From the Bay to the Cape, the going is very rough with what can be difficult river crossings and no optimum route. You pass over and between, what are by Scottish standards, low rounded hills. Eastwards, the view is bland by comparison with earlier stages being dominated by these low hills. Westwards, however, the rugged cliffs are never far away and across the Minch, weather permitting, the hills of Lewis are clearly visible some 60 kilometres away. The whole Stage is exposed to the westerlies and the rain can come at you in horizontal mode, but in sunlight the place is majestic.

At the Cape you really do feel an enormous sense of achievement as you stand and stare out from the top left-hand corner of Britain: due north, the next landfall is beyond the pole at Siberia, near the Bearing Straits; north-west are The Faroes, Iceland and Greenland beyond; due west is Labrador. Looking east, you see the north coast of Scotland, although you will need to ascend to the summit of Dùnan Mór to get the full view. Presumably, under very clear conditions, you will see Dunnet Head, beyond Thurso, about 90 kilometres (58 miles) away since, years ago, one clear beautiful summer evening, we were able to see Cape Wrath from Dunnet Head.

TWENTY FIRST STAGE

Blairmore to Cape Wrath

Sìthean na h-Iolaireich
230

Cnoc a' Gheodha Ruaidh

Sandwood Loch

Sandwood Bay

1km

Blairmore

We were researching at the Cape in the autumn of '97 when the lighthouse was still manned, but today it is automatic, requiring no day-to-day attention.

In high summer, at these latitudes, it never really gets dark at night. If you decide to take advantage of this, remember that you will suffer attack from clegs and midges.

We hope that you have enjoyed walking the route as much as we have enjoyed researching it. As there is no conventional road access at the end of this Stage, your last remaining problem will be to get back to 'civilisation'. We have offered a few suggestions in Appendix A.

21.1

ABC. Follow the defined track to its end at Loch á Mhuilinn. Rough in places.

D. The track degenerates to a path. Defined but very wet and boggy in places.

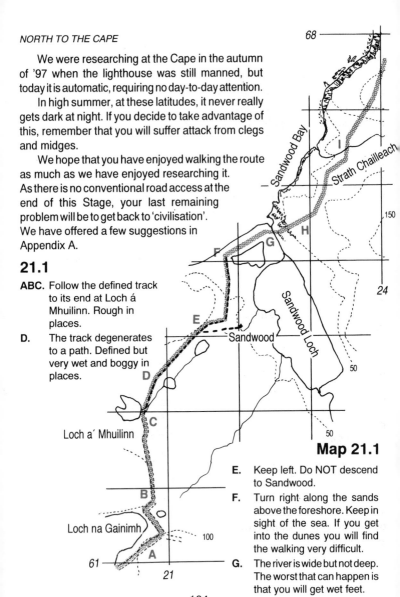

Map 21.1

E. Keep left. Do NOT descend to Sandwood.

F. Turn right along the sands above the foreshore. Keep in sight of the sea. If you get into the dunes you will find the walking very difficult.

G. The river is wide but not deep. The worst that can happen is that you will get wet feet.

H. Ascend steeply. Almost a scramble.

From now on, there is no best route. Make your own way by following the coastline, but do not get close to the high, dangerous cliffs. Immediate circumstances, such as terrain and weather, will decide your best route. Because there is no path, it is difficult and hence slow going. Do NOT underestimate the time required.

The route shown on the maps is the one we followed.

This is a difficult river crossing.

I. Do NOT attempt to cross near the sea as the river cascades down steeply to sea level.

21.2

Continue to make your own way.

There is another difficult river crossing.

A. Do NOT attempt to cross near the sea.

B. Steep. Almost a scramble. Keep away from the cliffs.

C. This crossing may be difficult after heavy rain.

D. Join the lane. Keep left and follow it to the lighthouse.

**CONGRATULATIONS —
YOU'VE MADE IT**

You have now the problem of getting away from Cape Wrath see Appendix A.

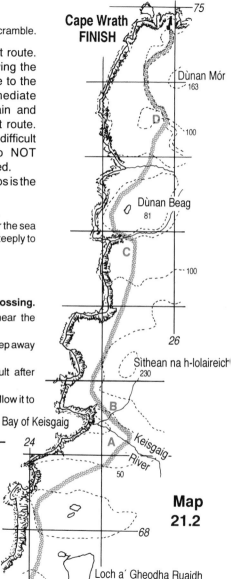

Cape Wrath
FINISH

Dùnan Mór
163

D

100

Dùnan Beag
81

C

100

26

Sithean na h-Iolaireich
230

B

Keisgaig-
River

Bay of Keisgaig

A

24

50

68

**Map
21.2**

Loch a' Gheodha Ruaidh

75

CAPE WRATH

As you trudge across the wet, peaty and featureless moorland on leaving Blairmore, you may very well wonder why you came so far. Keep going - your arrival at Sandwood Bay will lift up your spirits and brighten your whole outlook.

If Sandwood were anywhere else in the British Isles, it would be packed with holiday-makers, ice cream stalls, hot-dog stands and associated paraphernalia. As it is, the Bay is totally isolated. Long may it be so. Described by some as the most beautiful place in the Western Highlands, its name is a corruption of the Norse *Sand-vatn*, 'Sand-water'. You may be the only occupants of the one-and-a-half kilometre long beach, parallelled by rolling sand dunes and attendant fresh water loch. Enjoy the solitude. Enjoy the sound of the seabirds. Enjoy the Atlantic combers shattering themselves into mountains of spume against the firm white sand. But beware: for, while *The Good Beach Guide* lists the Bay as 'magnificent', swimming is described as 'very dangerous', due to the unpredictable tideflows and currents.

Off a small headland to the south of the bay, there rises an imposing red sandstone stack named Am Buachaille, 'The Herdsman'. To the north, seemingly only a stone's throw away, you can now see the lighthouse at Cape Wrath, but don't be deceived - you have some way to go yet. If you spend the night here, you may be lucky enough to see the mermaid. Sandwood Bay is the alleged site of the last recorded appearance in Great Britain of this delightful phenomenon. Perhaps she is guarding the many wrecks, buried metres deep in the dunes.

Reluctantly departing from this idyllic scene, your way ever northwards is rough due to the absence of paths. But it is not difficult. There are several long, narrow, steep sided clefts, known as geos. Formed by erosion in the coastal cliffs, the geos pose no real problems other than the possibility of having to go a few hundred metres inland to avoid the worst of the topographical drops and rises. If the westerlies bring rain during your journey, and they probably will, the showers will strike horizontally, straight off the Atlantic Ocean, almost flavoured with salt.

Three or four kilometres from Cape Wrath, you cross the peat-dark, rolling moor known as The Parph, a Gaelic corruption of the old Norse name for Cape Wrath, 'Hvarf' or 'turning-point'. The Cape marks the angle where the Viking ships altered course, veering south to enter The

Minch on their way to the West Coast of Scotland and the Hebrides. Having crossed the moor and joined the track, you will soon arrive at the most north-westerly point of the British Isles where, in the summer months, the sun hardly sets. At midnight it is possible to read even a newspaper at these latitudes.

Between 1724 and 1727, Daniel Defoe (1660 - 1731) wrote his three-volume travel book *A Tour through the Whole Island of Great Britain.* He described the North of Scotland in his Thirteenth and Last Letter and said that from John o' Groats:

"… the land, as it were, looking forward just against the Pole Star, and the Pole so elevated, that the tail of Ursa Major, or the Great Bear, is seen just in the zenith, or over your head; and the day is said to be eighteen hours long, that is to say, the sun is so long above the horizon: But the rest of the light is so far beyond a twilight, by reason of the smallness of the arch (sic) of that circle which the sun makes beneath the horizon, that it is clear and perfect day almost all the time; not forgetting without, that the dark nights take their turn with them in their season, and it is just as long in the winter."

Cape Wrath is not the most northerly point of the mainland of Britain. That distinction goes to Dunnet Head, and not John o' Groats as is popularly supposed. The Cape is, however, the most northerly point unreachable by motor transport (other than the minibus which runs from the Kyle of Durness to the Cape during the summer months). Long may this be the case, for its very remoteness is the essence of its charm.

As you come to the actual moment when you stand near the lighthouse savouring a well-earned sense of pride, you will feel as if you have reached the ends of the earth. There may be others present, having come by the easy way of ferry and minibus, but you will have done it the walkers' way. And the sense of achievement will be enormous. When the euphoria dies down, take a look around you and inspect the far horizons. Standing on Cape Wrath, you are at 122 metres above the waves. Nearby, Black Cliff is a sheer 260 metres from the swirling Atlantic. North, there's naught between you and the 2,700 kilometres distant North Pole except, perhaps, the odd ship working its way around the coast following the self same routes as the Viking long ships all those hundreds of years ago. To the east is Dunnet Head, some 90 kilometres away, beyond Thurso. A little to the north of Dunnet Head you can just detect the cliffs of Hoy, in the Orkneys some 95 kilometres away at a height of 348 metres. In exceptional weather conditions the low cliffs of North Rona rise mirage-like some 72 kilometres away; a mirage indeed, as the cliffs are only 100 metres high. Eighty kilometres south-west, as if pencilled on the horizon, one sees the low hills of Lewis in the Outer Hebrides. Much lower, in the sea below the Cape, are two low mounds. These rocks, over which the Atlantic swells in never-ending white flumes, are Am Bodach and A' Chailleach, 'The Old Man' and 'The Old Woman'.

Should the weather be venting its wrath on this aptly named cape, you will see none of these magical sights. But we have no doubt that you will return and return yet again to this bewitching place, just like those who fall under the spell of the Himalayan mountains in Nepal.

At the tip of the Cape, the (automatic) lighthouse stands foursquare against the elements. Built in 1827, the light can be seen for 40 kilometres and more. The adjacent buildings, long disused and now falling derelict, were once the homes of customs officers. The nearest habitation is at the bottom of the 11 kilometre track to the Kyle of Durness (accent on the 'ness'), across which a small foot passenger ferry plies from Keoldale. Haunt of anglers, The Cape Wrath Hotel offers the only accommodation in Keoldale. In Durness, three kilometres north-east, there are several hotels, many B & Bs, a Youth Hostel, a garage, bank, shops and Tourist Information Centre.

Well, you've done it. Your long adventure is at an end, You may have suffered deprivations. You may have been soaked through; you will certainly have got wet feet on more than one occasion. Exceptionally, you may have enjoyed good weather, at least some of the time; some excellent accommodation, food and drink. You may be feeling footsore and weary. You will certainly be a lot fitter than when you left Fort William all those days ago. Above all, we hope you will be elated and exhilarated having achieved what you set out to do.

Congratulations.

APPENDICES

A: LEAVING THE CAPE

Having arrived at The Cape, you will find neither public transport nor lighthouse keepers. You're on your own! However, we offer four different possibilities to help you leave The Cape:

1. Camp at Sandwood on the northerly leg of Stage Twenty-One. Leave your camp in situ whilst you walk to The Cape, and return to Sandwood for a second night. You will then have to walk to Kinlochbervie to catch the postbus which runs from Durness to Lairg. It leaves Kinlochbervie harbour at about 0905. It would be wise to check the latest postbus timetables with the Tourist Information Centre at Durness before you start this last Stage. Once in Lairg, you can continue your journey home on the rail network.

2. On arrival at The Cape, you will need a camping site. This may require a return to the burn, some 2 kilometres to the south. On the following day, walk back to Kinlochbervie.

3. If when you arrive at The Cape there are a few people around, this will mark the impending arrival of a minibus from The Kyle of Durness. You could wait with them, perhaps enjoying a snack from the (normally present) snack bar, catch the next minibus and cross the kyle on the ferry. There is an hotel at Keoldale, a few hundred metres from the ferry landing. Durness is 3 kilometres to the NE. From Durness the postbus runs Monday to Saturday. It leaves at about 0820, to arrive in Lairg (via Kinlochbervie) two-and-a-half hours later.

4. Before leaving Kinlochbervie, ring the ferryman, Mr Morrison (01971 511376), or the minibus owner, Mrs Makie (01971 511343/511287) and ask about ferry and minibus (approximate) times on your expected day and time of arrival at The Cape. In the unlikely event that you cannot get through to any of the above numbers, the Tourist Information Office at Durness (01971 511259) may be of help. The minibus and ferry both run, weather and tides permitting, from May to September.

B: PUBLIC RIGHTS OF WAY

Great Britain has a rich heritage of footpaths going back to prehistoric times. A network of footpaths was developed for trading purposes, especially in England and Wales. They linked centres where essentials, such as salt, flint and pottery, were to be found. The paths frequently followed high-level routes where travelling was easier. Low-lying land was usually boggy woodland. From the eighteenth century, people also began to use footpaths for recreational purposes. The books of Samuel Johnson, Jane Austen, the Brontës and Thomas Hardy, amongst others, contain many references to this new activity. Due to the sparsity of the population in Scotland, particularly in the West Highlands, the network of paths formed less quickly and was less developed. The original long-distance routes there were mainly military roads or drove roads for driving cattle to market.

Shortly after World War II, the British Government wanted to clarify the case law governing the use of paths. Laws were enacted In England and Wales to rationalize the whole system. As Scotland had, and still has, its own legal system, different laws apply.

Usually, rights of way in England and Wales come into being by 'dedication'. A landowner dedicates to the public a right of passage over an area of land. Sometimes the landowner does so expressly, but often the right of way will be acquired at common law. If a path has been used for a period of not less than 20 years, a right of way may be presumed to have been dedicated. It is not necessary for the same people to have used the route. It is necessary for members of the general public to have used the route, not just privileged groups such as tenants, employees or postal operatives. The path must also have been used openly and peaceably by members of the public as of right, without the permission, expressed or implicit, of the landowner.

As well as dedication and presumed dedication, rights of way in England, Scotland and Wales can be created 'by agreement' between landowners and county or local planning authorities. These routes may have restrictions placed on their use.

Rights of way in Scotland are also acquired by long use by the public (20 years or more), but the concept of 'dedication' by the landowner does not apply.

A right of way in Scotland must run from one public place to another. A 'public place' is one where the public have a legal right to be, for example, a public road, a church or ferry. Also, the right of way must follow a more or less dedicated route, which need not be visible on the ground.

On the Ordnance Survey (OS) 1:50,000 series maps (Landrangers), for

England and Wales, rights of way are indicated by short dashed red lines for footpaths and long dashed red lines for bridleways. The 1:25,000 series maps (Pathfinders and Outdoor Leisure) use short dashed green lines for right of way footpaths and long dashed green lines for bridleways. These maps carry the warning that the public rights of way are: 'Not Applicable in Scotland'. It is often claimed that there are no rights of way in Scotland. This is not true, but rights of way in Scotland are not distinguished from other paths on the OS 1:50,000 series and tracks are shown as long dashed black lines, but these may not be rights of way. Maps are of no assistance at all, in Scotland, in giving guidance about the status of any particular track or path.

In England, Scotland and Wales, a public right of way is a way over which the public has a right to pass and repass. Rights of way usually refer to unsurfaced tracks or paths and both are highways, just like the A1 or the M74. Local authorities in England and Wales have a duty to prepare definitive maps registering all rights of way within their boundaries. And if a right of way is shown on a definitive map, then the public has a right to walk on it. But, remember that OS maps showing rights of way can occasionally be inaccurate or simply out of date. In England and Wales, all rights of way should be signposted where they meet metalled roads, but often are not, and local authorities have powers to waymark paths along their route. They also have a duty to protect and assert public rights of way in their areas, for example by taking formal action to have obstructions removed.

The English and Welsh system of recording rights of way does not apply in Scotland. There are no officially registered rights of way there. However, many local authority planning departments keep records and maps of them. Also, the Scottish Rights of Way Society keeps records of the major routes and publishes maps of some of them for the use of its members. Some rights of way have been signposted by the Scottish Rights of Way Society or local authorities.

It is illegal for anyone in Great Britain to obstruct a right of way, for example with barbed wire, and it is the duty of the landowner (in Scotland, the local authority) to see that any such obstruction is removed. If a highway you are using is obstructed, you may remove just enough of the obstruction to allow you to pass. But, you must be careful and do the minimum of damage to the obstruction. If the path really is impassable, you are entitled to deviate and pass around it. However, if your deviation takes you onto land belonging to someone other than the person responsible for the obstruction, you may be trespassing.

A farmer may plough across a field path, but should reinstate its surface within two weeks (in Scotland 'as soon as maybe'), and paths running around field headlands should never be ploughed. Legally, by the way, if a right of way is shown across a cultivated field, you have the right to walk through whatever crop is planted. That has its problems, as anyone who has tried to walk through a crop of mature wheat, barley or, worse still, oilseed rape will know. If a crop in itself constitutes an impenetrable obstruction, you will have no option but to walk around its edges (legally).

Local authorities in England and Wales are responsible for maintaining the surface of paths, including bridges, whilst stiles and gates are the landowner's responsibility. Scottish landowners have no responsibility for maintaining a right of way, although the public may take up the task providing they do not damage any property. Local authorities may maintain paths if they wish, but they are not obliged to do so. But, as in England and Wales, they have a duty to maintain paths created by agreement.

Contrary to popular belief, there IS a law of trespass in Scotland. However, there is generally a welcome tolerance of access to many areas of land, particularly to moorlands and mountains. Popular routes within these areas, or to the summits of some hills or mountains, are not necessarily rights of way.

During the stalking season (mainly September/October, but could be at other times also), signs may be displayed on some estates in Scotland advising walkers to discuss their proposed route with the estate's Head Stalker before proceeding. The signs imply that alternative routes may be offered, to avoid disturbing shooting operations.

Rights of Access, which are not the same as rights of way, are currently the subject of much debate. In 1947, a special committee on footpaths and access recommended to the then Minister for Town and Country Planning that a public right of access should be extended to all open country, with certain exceptions. But the Minister was swayed by representations from landowners and the resulting National Parks and Access to the Countryside Act 1949 provided for access agreements to be negotiated site by site. Few such agreements have been reached since 1949.

There is an age-old tradition in Scotland of free access to mountains and glens. The tradition is not protected by law, but Scottish walkers and visitors to Scotland place tremendous value on this 'freedom to roam'. The freedom is sometimes challenged in areas where estate owners wish to 'preserve their privacy'. The Scots enjoy the freedom to roam at the discretion of the landowner. The English and Welsh hardly enjoy any such freedom, although their rights of way are more clearly defined.

At the time of writing, the whole subject of rights of access was being debated in Government circles. The then ruling Parliamentary Party appeared to be in favour of the freedom to roam, and Landowners' and Walkers' organisations were being consulted. It is to be hoped that the resultant Acts of Parliament will maintain current access agreements and legally open up the countryside for the benefit and enjoyment of all.

C: USEFUL ADDRESSES

Backpackers Club
49 Lyndhurst Road
EXMOUTH EX8 3DS
01395 265159

British Mountaineering Council
177-179 Burton Road
MANCHESTER M20 2BB
0161 445 4747

British Waterways
Willow Grange
Church Road
WATFORD
Herts WD1 3QA
01923 226422

Camping & Caravanning Club Ltd
Greenfields House
Westwood Way
COVENTRY CV4 8JH
01203 694995

Country Landowners Association
16 Belgrave Square
LONDON SW1X 8PQ
0171 235 0511

Cyclists Touring Club
Cotterell House
69 Meadrow
GODALMING
Surrey GU7 3HS
01438 417217

Farm Holiday Bureau
National Agricultural Centre
STONELEIGH PARK
Warks CV8 2LZ
01203 696699

Forestry Commission
231 Corstophine Road
EDINBURGH EH12 7AT
0131 334 0303

Inland Waterways Association
114 Regents Park Road
LONDON NW1 8QU
0171 586 2510/2556

Long Distance Walkers Association
C/O Les Maple
21 Upcroft
WINDSOR
Berks SL4 3NH
01753 866685

Mountain Bothies Association
Publicity Officer
Ted Butcher
26 Rycroft Avenue
Deeping St James
PETERBOROUGH PE6 8NT

Mountaineering Council of Scotland
4a St Catherine's Road
PERTH PH1 5SE
01738 638227

National Trust for Scotland
5 Charlotte Square
EDINBURGH EH2 4DU
0131 226 5922

Ordnance Survey
Romsey Road
Maybush
SOUTHAMPTON
Hants SO16 4GU
01703 792000

Ramblers' Association Scotland
Crusader House
Haig Business Park
MARKINCH
Fife KY7 7AQ
01592 611177

Scottish Rights of Way Society
John Cotton Business Centre
10 Sunnyside
EDINBURGH EH7 5RA
0131 652 2937

Scottish Tourist Board
23 Ravelston Terrace
EDINBURGH EH4 3EU
0131 332 2433

Scottish Youth Hostels Association
7 Glebe Crescent
STIRLING FK8 2JA
01786 451181

D: RELEVANT OS MAPS

Landranger (1:50,000)

41	—	Ben Nevis
40	—	Loch Shiel
33	—	Loch Alsh & Glen Shiel
25	—	Glen Carron
19	—	Gairloch & Ullapool Area
20	—	Ben Dearg & Surrounding Area
16	—	Lairg, Loch Shin & Surrounding Area
15	—	Loch Assynt & Surrounding Area
9	—	Cape Wrath, Durness & Scourie

Pathfinder/Outdoor Leisure (1:25,000)

9 & 10	—	Cuillin and Torridon Hills

E: PLACE NAMES

Many Highland place names are derived from Gaelic or Norse origins. Here are a few words and meanings, which may help with your map reading:

Aber	Mouth or confluence of a river
Abhainn	River
Achadh (achug)	Field
Airidh	Shieling
Allt	Stream, water
Aonach (aynach)	Ridge
Ard	High, lofty
Ban	White
Beag (beg)	Small
Beallach (byallach)	Mountain pass
Bidean (beejan)	Pinnacle
Bun	River mouth
Cairn	Heap of stones used as a marker
Cleugh	Ravine
Cnoc (knock)	Hill
Coille (collu)	Wood
Coirre (corru)	Hollow in the hills
Creag	Rock
Dhu	Black
Dun (doon)	Fort
Eilean (aylan)	Island
Garbh	Rough, rugged
Gill	Ravine, watercourse
Glas	Grey
Gleann (glyown)	Glen
Gorm	Blue, green
Inbhir (inver)	Confluence of waters
Kin	Head
Kirk	Church
Kyle	Narrow strait of water
Lagan	Little hollow
Liathe	Grey
Linne	Pool, waterfall
Loch	Freshwater lake, fjord
Machair	Fertile plain near shore

Mam	Rounded hill
Monadh (monug)	Hill, moor
Mor	Great, extensive
Ness	Headland
Rannoch	Bracken
Rudha (rooa)	Promontory
Sgur	Rocky peak
Sheugh	Ditch
Shieling	Temporary summer dwelling
Sloch	Pit
Srath (sra)	Strath, wide valley
Stob	Pointed hill
Tarbert	Isthmus
Tullach	Small Hill
Uamh	Cave
Uisge (uushku)	Water, river

BIBLIOGRAPHY

Of the many reference and other books used during the preparation of this publication, the authors would, in particular, like to record the following:

Adam J.S. *Gaelic Wordbook*   Chambers 1995

Angus S. et al   *AA/OS Scottish Highlands Guide* AA/OS 1994

Bartholomew J. (Ed) *Scottish Hill Tracks* (*)   The Scottish Rights of Way Society 1995

Brook D. & Hinchliffe P. *The Alternative Pennine Way* Cicerone Press 1992

Brook D. & Hinchliffe P. *The Alternative Coast to Coast* Cicerone Press 1995

Church C. & Dagg C. *Ullapool and the North-West of Scotland*

Chris Church 1996

Clapham F.M. (Ed) *Factbook of British History*   Rainbow Books 1993

Forest J. *Introducing Fort William & Lochaber*   Firtree Publishing Ltd 1995

Gordon S. *Highways and Byways in the West Highlands*

Macmillan & Co 1935

Gunn G. & Spankie M. *The Highland Clearances*

Wayland Publishers Ltd 1993

Hutton G. *Caledonian The Monster Canal*   Richard Stenlake 1991

Isaacs A. & Monk J. (Ed) *The Illustrated Dictionary of British Heritage*
University of Cambridge 1993

McKnight H. *The Shell Book of Inland Waterways*   David & Charles 1978

McOwen *Tartans The Facts and Myths*   Jarrold Publishing 1996

Milroy W. *Malt Whisky Almanac*   Lochar Publishing 1987

Morrice P. *The Schweppes Guide to Scotch*   Alphabooks 1983

Murray W.H. *The Companion Guide to The West Highlands of Scotland*
Collins 1968

Newby E. & Petry D. *Wonders of Britain*   Hodder and Stoughton 1968

Prager C. (Ed) *The Rambler's Yearbook & Accommodation Guide*
The Ramblers' Association 1998

Speight G. (Ed) *The New Shell Guide to Britain*   Ebury Press 1985

Stewart K. *Crofts and Crofting*   Mercat Press 1980

Taylor W. *The Military Roads of Scotland*   House of Lochar 1996

Ward J.O. (Ed) *The Oxford Companion to Music*
Oxford University Press 1988

Warren J. *A Feast of Scotland*   Lomond Books 1979

Westacott H.D. *The Walkers Handbook*   Penguin Books 1980

Wightman A. *Who Owns Scotland*   Canongate Books 1996

Williams P. *Hill Walking*   Pelham Books Ltd 1979

(*) *Scottish Hill Tracks*, published by The Scottish Rights of Way Society, proved to be particularly useful to us during our research.

The dates are those of the editions consulted.

In addition, many town guides, tourist guides, and brochures were read. Our appreciation goes to all the (often anonymous) authors and publishers who compiled them.

NOTE ON THE ILLUSTRATIONS

The illustrations are reproductions of wood engravings i.e. prints made from wooden blocks with the image engraved on the end grain. Most are reproduced at approximately the size of the original prints except for some which have been reduced.

PRINTED BY CARNMOR PRINT & DESIGN, LONDON ROAD, PRESTON, LANCS.